CHRISTIANITY
IS NOT A
RELIGION.
IT IS
RELATIONSHIP

DANIEL MURPHY

BOOKS Where Best Sellers
Are Made

Author: Daniel Murphy

ABN: 94 010 702 326
Email: dan@1770group.com.au

First Published April 2024

The moral rights of the author have been asserted.

ISBN: 978-0-9756643-6-0

Disclaimer:

The opinions presented in this book solely belong to the author and may not necessarily align with the perspectives of any religious entity, group, or individual. The author recognizes that the topics addressed may be sensitive to certain readers. Neither the author nor the publisher assume responsibility for any consequences resulting from the interpretation or application of the material contained herein.

CONTENTS

JESUS IS THE TREE OF LIFE

HIS BLOOD BYPASSES RELIGION

STRAIGHT TO RELATIONSHIP

INTRODUCTION:

BEFORE THE BEGINNING

God's Plan and What Went Wrong

The Bible is unlike any other book. It is *alive*. The Bible is the living Word of God. It is Jesus, and he speaks the TRUTH to us as a living, breathing manual for our life. No other book begins before the creation of our universe and carries us beyond the very end.

OMNISCIENT- ALL-KNOWING

Time, as we understand it, began with the creation of our universe. God was there before that and held the creation plan in His mind. It was not just the blueprint for how He would create the world, but like a Master Author, He prerecorded all of history before it unfolded and set it in stone so that His plan is unalterable, even by humanity.

He gave the record to humanity through His prophets, those holding the pen of the Holy Spirit, and they recorded His Word. This is our Bible.

The Creator has revealed to us the end of His account and shown us the eternal and final state of all created beings. Each of us will live with God in His eternal home if we have been enabled to do so. He has given us His Word so we can learn how to live on Earth and enter that state of being. Revelation 21:1-4 says:

> [1] Now I saw a new Heaven and a new Earth, for the first Heaven and the first Earth had passed away. Also, there was no more sea. [2] Then I, John, saw the holy city, New Jerusalem, coming down out of Heaven from God, prepared as a bride adorned for her husband. [3] And I heard a loud voice from Heaven saying, "Behold, the tabernacle of God *is* with men, and He will dwell with them, and they shall be His people. God Himself will be with them *and be* their God. [4] And God will wipe away every tear from their eyes; there shall be no more death, nor sorrow, nor crying. There shall be no more pain, for the former things have passed away." (NKJV)

Then verse 7 tells us: "The one who conquers will have this heritage, and I will be his God, and he will be my son."

And Revelation 21:22-24 says:

> [22] "But I saw no temple in it, for the Lord God Almighty and the Lamb are its temple. [23] The city had no need of the sun or of the moon to shine in it, for the glory of God illuminated it. The Lamb *is* its light. [24] And the nations of those who are saved shall walk in its light, and the kings of the Earth bring their glory and honor into it." (NKJV)

This is phenomenal news, but these Scriptures raise many questions that only one book in the whole world can answer. The book's Author has recorded His response through the prophets and apostles by His Holy Spirit. Perhaps you already have the questions forming:

1. What has gone wrong with God's "good" creation?

2. How did sin come into this initially pure universe?

3. How did mankind get separated from the Eternal Creator Who so obviously loves us, and how did we lose His Kingdom, throwing away not only Eden but our whole world, losing our precious relationship with our Maker and Father?

4. What can be done to restore our citizenship in His Kingdom and become partakers of the final state of being so clearly written about?

5. How can we communicate with the God Who does not register to any of our five senses? In other words, how does finite man commune and communicate with an Infinite Spirit?

6. How do we even begin to understand His Being – One Who is so high above us in nature?

7. How do we hope to discover how God feels about us as His creation?

8. What will eternal life be like in an immortal body living in the presence of the Eternal Creator?

The wonderful and devastatingly underappreciated good news is that in the Bible, every major event that has ever and will ever occur concerning God and His creation is recorded for all to see. The Redemptive Story and the plan of salvation are meticulously laid bare for anyone to grasp—a step-by-step guide to how God will fulfill His wonderful plan. Each of us must continually seek His face for the unveiling of that plan and our place in it. These undeniable truths from Scripture are authenticated repeatedly by the fulfillment of hundreds of prophecies. The two most extraordinary prophetic events recorded are the First Coming of Christ and the Second Coming of Christ. The first has been gloriously fulfilled with angelic worship and announcement in a humble manger. We breathlessly await the Second Coming of Christ, our Messiah, having read several hundred prophecies in the Divine Scriptures that He will come again as surely as He came the first time.

Look at the last book of the Bible, Revelation, to see what Christ Jesus tells us of the plans of God:

"I am the Alpha and the Omega, the Beginning and the End…Who is and Who was and Who is to come, the Almighty!" (Rev 1:8)

"And behold, I am coming quickly, and My reward is with Me, to give to everyone according to his work. I am the Alpha and the Omega, the Beginning and the End, the First and the Last." (Rev 22:12-13)

The men and women we learn of in the Bible were far from perfect, but the heroes of the faith had one thing in common that made them heroes: No matter their faults and failures, "They Loved the Lord their God with all of their soul, mind, strength and heart." **These loved God for Himself alone, not for what they could get or what He could do for them.**

Scholars believe the Book of Job is the earliest manuscript written and recorded. Why would the Holy Spirit see that it was written first? Because it is the story about one man's love for his God for Himself alone and is the only thing that matters in life.

That we should reflect the *imago dei,* the image of God, and grow to become more and more like our Father and Maker is testified to by Scripture upon Scripture.

At any point in the history of creation, if man had only stopped to look into the plan of the omniscient God, how different would things have been? Particularly today, what is needed is this "looking." Now more than ever, as our race is on the brink of self-annihilation, we keep looking for solutions to all our problems in the wrong places. We are seekers of truth, but we are blind seekers! We seek the answers in man when the answers can only be found in the One Who created us, the One Who is omniscient, the One Who will in no way be thwarted in His ultimate good plan to bring things to their completion.

Many Christians believe that this world will end, and Christ will return, but what they often miss in the plain text of Scripture is that God knows all things and knew from the very start that Satan would rebel against Him. The LORD knew that His Son, Adam, would rebel and that all of us, his descendants, would rebel against the One we were created to love completely. God, the Almighty, knew we would turn against Him, His Plan, and His Son. El Shaddai (God Almighty) could see right through it all and hold clearly in His mind as though it had all already happened through to the glorious New Heaven and Earth, the Holy New Jerusalem in the renewed Universe created for His glory! Our Father could see us vividly in our final eternal state of being in pure light with Him, in Him, and for Him, the all in all.

What does our Father want? Why has He revealed Himself and given us the mind of Christ to comprehend and know what angels long to know? In short, He wants us to look past ourselves and the created things to see only Him, and He wants us to experience the blessing and joy of love for Him for Who He is, because when all is said and done (a fairly big statement), what we will receive as our ultimate reward is "Him!"

Sadly, we are woefully short-sighted and small-minded to want the worthless nothingness of this world instead. Since eternity past, God has had a longing for us that we would choose to look past Eden, which was only meant to be one step of His plan, to look past our present age, and even to look past the 1000 years of the millennium to come when Jesus returns gloriously to Earth to rule and reign with His saints, and to look eagerly to our final destination, the end goal for humanity for which the Lamb slain since the foundation of the world died and rose again.

God's deep and mysterious plan that has been unfolding for thousands of years has been for an all-encompassing re*lationship* between Him and us, His children, that He should be "all in all." (1 Cor 15) We understand the Garden of Eden to be a wonderful paradise lost, but man's existence there pales in comparison to what God ultimately had and has in store for us in the final epoch. Even those of us who will reign for 1000 years with Christ will not know the level of intimacy desired by the Eternal Creator, Father, Son, and Holy Spirit for His children, His bride.

There is no level of relationship deep and intimate enough for our Father except what has been revealed to us in Revelation that will occur in the New Heavens and the New Earth! (Rev 21, 22) Astonishingly, God has revealed His plan to humankind, and we tragically take it for granted! We need to take the time to go and see what His Word says, to seek Him so we can seek His Word *with Him.*

Ephesians 1:4-5, and then 9-11 says:

> [4] Just as He chose us in Him before the foundation of the world, that we should be holy and without blame before Him in love, [5] having predestined us to adoption as sons by Jesus Christ to Himself, according to the good pleasure of His will, [9] having made known to us the mystery of His will, according to His good pleasure which He purposed in Himself, that in the dispensation of the fullness of the times He might gather in one all things in Christ, both which are in Heaven and which are on Earth—in Him. [10] In Him also we have obtained an inheritance, being predestined according to the purpose of Him Who works all things according to the counsel of His will.

How Did Evil Get into Our World?

Before God in Heaven created all things, He dwelled in His Eternal Heavenly Courts, a place beyond anything we have ever seen or could imagine. With all majesty and glory, the Father ruled His kingdom from His high and royal throne, of which all the grandest and most opulent earthly kingdoms and throne rooms are a poor and dim reflection.

God the Father proclaimed that because He had One unique, begotten Son He loved so dearly, He desired a larger family that would be just like Yeshua (the actual Hebrew Name for Jesus), His Eternal Son. This created Being would be granted the freedom of will to choose to love Him for Himself alone, not for what He could give them, but for Who He is. They could choose to be just like their "Dad" in every possible way to reflect Him and His glory. God, Who would declare that no other image should be graven of Him, created His image in humanity to reflect Him.

GOD proclaimed to all the heavenly host that "WE are going to make them, this new creation, in OUR IMAGE and they will be second only to US in all of creation." (paraphrase of Genesis 1:28)

(At the end of this story in the book of Revelation, we see similar proclamations being made to bring all the creation we now see and know to an end.)

At the announcement of this declaration, Satan blurted his own statement, "That was the final straw!"

Satan, Lucifer, was once called Light-Bearer, Shining One, and Morning Star. These accolades came before his pride-driven rebellion when his ego refused to be set lower than this new being (man). That once beautiful being rebelled, and in an extraordinary turn of events, he convinced one-third of all the other angels to abandon Heaven in rebellion with him.

Lucifer is driven by his hell-bent desire to destroy humanity, God's image-bearing children, and he hates and detests us with such fiery passion that his entire mission in his long supernatural life is to rob GOD of HIS children. It is the very reason this world is in the dark state it is in, ruled by death and destruction.

FREEWILL

We have been hoodwinked. We have been taught that God, Who gave us the wonderful gift of freewill, wants to remove it. On the contrary, nothing could be further from the truth. The adversary who robs and destroys is behind this deception. It is Satan who would steal the gift of freewill and cheat us out of the true love of and from God.

I can prove this easily by providing examples of where our freewill is stolen. Exhibit A is our mobile phone, tablet, or other device. Try taking them away from the average person for just one day and witness the anxiety. Most people are unable to say "No" to their devices. They do not have the free will to deny themselves these pieces of plastic, and in many cases, their lives are being destroyed. But this is not how God created us to function as autonomous stewards of our lives.

For others, it is drugs, alcohol, cigarettes, pornography, or even food. "Their end is destruction, their god is their belly, and they glory in their shame, with minds set on earthly things." (Phil 3:19 ESV) Manufactured items grab us and dictate life to us. We've been robbed of our innocence, and our freewill to say "NO" is lost.

But in Christ, we can regain the freewill that was part of our original design. To be completely free is to be free from "self," that is to be selfless. It comes only one way: through and by Christ. Read 1 Corinthians 13, the great chapter on love.

> [1] If I speak in the tongues of men and of angels, but have not love, I am a noisy gong or a clanging cymbal. [2] And if I have prophetic powers, and understand all mysteries and all knowledge, and if I have all faith, to remove mountains, but

have not love, I am nothing. [3] If I give away all I have, and if I deliver up my body to be burned but have not love, I gain nothing.

[4] Love is patient and kind; love does not envy or boast; it is not arrogant [5] or rude. It does not insist on its own way; it is not irritable or resentful; [6] it does not rejoice at wrongdoing but rejoices with the truth. [7] Love bears all things, believes all things, hopes all things, endures all things.

[8] Love never ends. As for prophecies, they will pass away; as for tongues, they will cease; as for knowledge, it will pass away. [9] For we know in part, and we prophesy in part, [10] but, when the perfect comes, the partial will pass away. [11] When I was a child, I spoke like a child, I thought like a child, I reasoned like a child. When I became a man, I gave up childish ways. [12] For now we see in a mirror dimly, but then face to face. Now I know in part; then I shall know fully, even as I have been fully known.

[13] So now faith, hope, and love abide, these three; but the greatest of these is love.

This selflessness is an unthinkable way of life for most people. What few comprehend is that Paul is giving the very description of *freedom*. Look now at our modern world and the number of things that are forced upon us, the things we are told we must accept. Who is behind this stripping away of our God-given freedom of will? The adversary! He won't be finished with us until we are controlled by a microchip in our bodies dictating every facet of our lives. Only then will the theft be ultimate, and only then will our lives have been stolen from the One Who loves us, our Creator!

Consider the dreadful names for our adversary, the tempter (Mt 4:1-3), the accuser of the brethren (Rev 12:10), murder and father of lies (Jn 8:44), Beelzebub, prince of demons (Mk 2:1-3), Belial, evil personified (2 Cor 6:15), the dragon (Rev 12:9).

And Satan is not alone. A hierarchy of demons serves him. A demon (δαίμων) is an evil spirit, a fallen angel. Before the creation of the world, these demons served and worshiped God until, under the leadership of Lucifer (Satan), they rebelled against GOD. Now, night and day, they carry out their program of stealing, killing, and destroying God's children. Remember why they rebelled: because God had dared to create a higher being, higher because we were created in God's very image, a fact that brings hatred from the demons consumed with pride.

Isaiah promises us that one day, we will look upon Satan in bewilderment as to why such an insignificant being could do so much damage when, in fact, he had to do very little but leave us fallen humans to our own devices.

Isaiah 14:12-17 NKJV says:

> [12] "How you are fallen from Heaven,
> O Lucifer, son of the morning!
> *How* you are cut down to the ground,
> you who weakened the nations!
>
> [13] For you have said in your heart:
> 'I will ascend into Heaven,
> I will exalt my throne above the stars of God;
> I will also sit on the mount of the congregation
> on the farthest sides of the north;
>
> [14] I will ascend above the heights of the clouds;
> I will be like the Most High.'
>
> [15] Yet you shall be brought down to Sheol,
> to the lowest depths of the Pit.
>
> [16] Those who see you will gaze at you,
> *and* consider you, *saying:*

'*Is* this the man who made the Earth tremble,
who shook kingdoms,

[17] who made the world as a wilderness
and destroyed its cities,
who did not open the house of his prisoners?'"

"How you are fallen from Heaven, O Lucifer (Day Star), son of the morning! How you are cut down to the ground, You who weakened the nations!"

It appears from Scripture that there is a demonic prince over each nation that rules under the prince of this world (Satan) and oversees the demonic forces in each country, strategically carrying out his work. Daniel 10:9-21 says:

[9] Yet I heard his words; and while I heard his words, I was in a deep sleep on my face, with my face to the ground.

[10] Suddenly, a hand touched me, which made me tremble on my knees and *on* the palms of my hands. [11] And he said to me, "O Daniel, man greatly beloved, understand the words that I speak to you, and stand upright, **for I have now been sent to you.**" While he was speaking this word to me, I stood trembling. [12] Then he said to me, "Do not fear, Daniel, for from the first day that you set your heart to understand, and to humble yourself before your God, your words were heard; and I have come because of your words. [13] **But the prince of the Kingdom of Persia withstood me twenty-one days; and behold, Michael, one of the chief princes, came to help me, for I had been left alone there with the kings of Persia.** [14] Now, I have come to make you understand what will happen to your people in the latter days, for the vision *refers* to *many* days yet *to come.*"

[15] When he had spoken such words to me, I turned my face toward the ground and became speechless. [16] And suddenly, *one* having the likeness of the sons of men touched my lips; then I opened my mouth and spoke, saying to him who stood before me, "My lord, because of the vision my sorrows have overwhelmed me, and I have retained no strength. [17] For how can this servant of my lord talk with you, my lord? As for me, no strength remains in me now, nor is any breath left in me."

[18] Then again, *the one* having the likeness of a man touched me and strengthened me. [19] And he said, "O man greatly beloved, fear not! Peace *be* to you; be strong, yes, be strong!" So, when he spoke to me, I was strengthened, and said, "Let my lord speak, for you have strengthened me." [20] Then he said, "Do you know why I have come to you? **And now I must return to fight with the prince of Persia; and when I have gone forth, indeed the prince of Greece will come." [21] But I will tell you what is noted in the Scripture of Truth. (No one upholds me against these, except Michael your prince.)**

Most would agree that of all the ways man can sin, pride is the worst, simply because this was the sin of Satan. A holy and perfect God cannot abide sin, and He has done everything possible to provide for our cleansing from sin. But the sin that disgusts Him most is pride and its sister, self-righteousness. Some would be surprised to know that Proverbs 6:16-19 tells us:

[16] There are six things that the LORD hates,
   seven that are an abomination to him:
[17] haughty eyes, a lying tongue,
   and hands that shed innocent blood,
[18] a heart that devises wicked plans,
   feet that make haste to run to evil,
[19] a false witness who breathes out lies,
   and one who sows discord among brothers.

"Haughty eyes" or "A proud look" top the list. We are told over and over in the epistles, the letters in the New Testament, to beware in these last days of what will creep into our churches and to recognize them for who and what they are: They are bodies of pride, reflections of all that is opposite to the character of CHRIST as identified in 1 Corinthians 13 (see above). They will be proud, intolerant of truth, self-seeking, envious, rude, selfish, and easily provoked. The damage they can do to the body of Christ is beyond measure. Consider part 1 Corinthians 13 if we read it in the opposite way and use it to describe pride:

> Pride is **not** patient and **not** kind; pride **envies and boasts**; it is **arrogant and rude**. Pride **insists on its own way**; it is **irritable and resentful**; [6] it **rejoices at wrongdoing** but **does not rejoice** with the truth.

2 Corinthians 11:13-15 says:

> [13] For such *are* false apostles, deceitful workers, transforming themselves into apostles of Christ. [14] And no wonder! For Satan Himself transforms Himself into an angel of light. [15] Therefore, *it is* no great thing if his ministers also transform themselves into ministers of righteousness, whose end will be according to their works.

And as Paul writes to his protege, Timothy in 1 Timothy 4:1-2:

> [1] Now the Spirit expressly says that in later times some will depart from the faith by devoting themselves to deceitful spirits and teachings of demons, [2] through the insincerity of liars whose consciences are seared…

As the Day of the Lord comes nearer and nearer, these liars and false apostles will become more and more obvious as their character will be directly opposite to that of Christ. But to identify them, rather than deteriorate with them, we must stay continually in intimate relationship with the Savior. The more we abide in light and in Him, the more we will recognize and be repulsed by the darkness. When we walk in the Spirit and have the mind of Christ, we will despise what God despises. What are abominations to Him will be abominations to us. The false prophets, the wolves, and the servants of Satan will not be able to deceive us. If we do not abide in Christ, we will fall with them. 2 Peter 2 casts a dire warning:

[1] But there were also **false prophets** among the people, even **as there will be false teachers among you,** who will secretly bring in **destructive heresies,** even denying the Lord Who bought them, and bring on themselves swift destruction. [2] And **many will follow their destructive ways**, because of whom the way of truth will be blasphemed. [3] By covetousness **they will exploit you with deceptive words**; for a long time their judgment has not been idle, and their destruction does not slumber.

[4] For **if God did not spare the angels who sinned**, but cast them down to Hell and delivered them into chains of darkness, to be reserved for judgment; [5] and did not spare the ancient world, but saved Noah, one of eight people, a preacher of righteousness, bringing in the flood on the world of the ungodly; [6] and turning the cities of Sodom and Gomorrah into ashes, condemned them to destruction, making them **an example to those who afterward would live ungodly**; [7] and delivered righteous Lot, who was oppressed by the filthy conduct of the wicked [8] (for that righteous man, dwelling among them, **tormented his righteous soul from day to day by seeing and hearing their lawless deeds**)— [9] then the Lord knows how to deliver the godly out of temptations and **to reserve the unjust under punishment** for the day of judgment, [10] and especially those who walk according to the flesh in the lust of uncleanness and despise authority. They are presumptuous, self-willed. They are not afraid to **speak evil of**

dignitaries, [11] Whereas angels, who are greater in power and might, do not bring a reviling accusation against them before the Lord.

[12] But these, like natural brute beasts **made to be caught and destroyed, speak evil** of the things they do not understand, and **will utterly perish in their own corruption**, [13] and will receive the **wages of unrighteousness**, as those who count it pleasure to carouse in the daytime. They are spots and blemishes, **carousing in their own deceptions while they feast with you,** [14] having eyes full of adultery and that cannot cease from sin, enticing unstable souls. They have a heart trained in covetous practices and are accursed children. [15] They have **forsaken the right way and gone astray,** following the way of Balaam the son of Beor, who loved the wages of unrighteousness; [16] but, he was rebuked for his iniquity: a dumb donkey speaking with a man's voice restrained the madness of the prophet.

[17] These are wells without water, clouds carried by a tempest, for whom is **reserved the blackness of darkness forever.**

[18] For when they speak great swelling words of emptiness, they allure through the lusts of the flesh, through lewdness, the ones who have actually escaped from those who live in error. [19] While they promise them liberty, **they themselves are slaves of corruption**; for by whom a person is overcome, by him also he is brought into bondage. [20] For if, after they have escaped the pollutions of the world through the knowledge of the Lord and Savior Jesus Christ, they are again entangled in them and overcome, the latter end is worse for them than the beginning. [21] **For it would have been better for them not to have known the way of righteousness, than having known it, to turn from the holy commandment** delivered to them. [22] But it has happened to them according to the true proverb: "A dog

returns to his own vomit," and, "A sow, having washed, to her wallowing in the mire."

There is no question that this will be a feature of the Lord's recompense. May none of us be found on the wrong side. May all who read this turn fiercely away from sin and apostasy and turn their loved ones away.

Jude 1:6-7 tells us:

> [6] And the angels who did not keep their proper domain, but left their own abode, He has reserved in everlasting chains under darkness for the judgment of the great day; [7] as Sodom and Gomorrah, and the cities around them in a similar manner to these, having given themselves over to sexual immorality and gone after strange flesh, are set forth as an example, suffering the vengeance of eternal fire.

Consider it: Lucifer was in Heaven with God the Father, the Son, and the Spirit. He was in a lofty position and traded it for destruction. It is tragic to witness his fall, but also a great relief to see his final judgment and demise after all his violent and evil crimes against God and humanity. He will have no say, sway, or power in the eternal kingdom, not even over himself. "He was and is and now is not."

The tragedies and disasters we are currently witnessing on our planet are the playing out and fulfillment of these prophecies in Scripture, which we see in Revelation 12. What other explanation can be given for the unprecedented explosion of evil that is now gripping our world besides these writings? Revelation 12:3-9 says:

> [3] And another sign appeared in Heaven: **behold, a great, fiery red dragon having seven heads and ten horns, and seven diadems on his heads.** [4] His tail drew a third of the stars of Heaven and threw them to the Earth. And the dragon stood

before the woman who was ready to give birth, to devour her Child as soon as it was born. [5] She bore a male Child Who was to rule all nations with a rod of iron. And her Child was caught up to God and His throne. [6] Then the woman fled into the wilderness, where she has a place prepared by God, that they should feed her there one thousand two hundred and sixty days.

[7] And war broke out in Heaven: Michael and his angels fought with the dragon; **and the dragon and his angels fought,** [8] **but, they did not prevail, nor was a place found for them in Heaven any longer.** [9] So the great dragon was cast out, that serpent of old, called the Devil and Satan, who deceives the whole world; he was **cast to the Earth, and his angels were cast out with him.**

No matter what we see as events unfold in the coming days, always remember there is an end to Satan and his horde, and he has no place in eternity except destruction.

"The devil, who deceived them, was cast into the lake of fire and brimstone where the beast and the false prophet are. And they will be tormented day and night forever and ever." (Rev 20:10)

The goal of this book is to make clear what is given in Scripture. I will not venture to say more than what God has revealed and what I have seen with my own eyes in the clash of kingdoms. I am a witness, and God help me if I do not proclaim the gospel of truth and the things that are to come. My hope and prayer is that anyone who reads this will be moved beyond their ability to resist the call of God to walk forever in His eternal light, to surrender to the rule and reign of His Son, the King of kings and the Lord of lords, to live in the pure light and love of the One Who created them for His glory and for a loving relationship beyond anything that in our limited and sinful flesh we can comprehend. By grace through faith, we can have some dim understanding by the dim reflection granted to us by the Spirit. Still, I know with all my being by what I have already witnessed that:

> [9b] "What no eye has seen, nor ear heard,
> nor the heart of man imagined,
> what God has prepared for those who love him"—

> [10] These things God has revealed to us through the Spirit. For the Spirit searches everything, even the depths of God. [11] For who knows a person's thoughts except the spirit of that person, which is in him? So also no one comprehends the thoughts of God except the Spirit of God. [12] Now we have received not the spirit of the world, but the Spirit who is from God, that we might understand the things freely given us by God. [13] And we impart this in words not taught by human wisdom but taught by the Spirit, interpreting spiritual truths to those who are spiritual.

> [14] The natural person does not accept the things of the Spirit of God, for they are folly to him, and he is not able to understand them because they are spiritually discerned. [15] The spiritual person judges all things but, is himself to be judged by no one. [16] "For who has understood the mind of the Lord so as to instruct him?" But we have the mind of Christ. (1 Cor 2:9b-16)

May we all read these words with "the mind of Christ" and become witnesses so the bride of Christ could be adorned for His glorious return and the End of Days.

But the world, we are told in Revelation 13, will worship "the Abomination that makes desolate" and pay the price and suffer the consequences of this detestable worship (as mentioned in Revelation 16:2).

> [2] So, the first went and poured out his bowl upon the Earth, and a foul and loathsome sore came upon the men who had the mark of the beast and those who worshiped his image.

"Everyone living on Earth will worship it except those whose names are written in the Book of Life belonging to the Lamb slaughtered before the world was founded." (Revelation of Yeshua to Yochanan 13:8 CJB)

"All who dwell on the Earth will worship him, whose names have not been written in the Book of Life of the Lamb slain from the foundation of the world." (Rev 13:8 NKJV)

CHAPTER 1:

WHO IS GOD AND WHO ARE WE?

Is Your God Too Small, and Have You Made Yourself Too Big?

"Christianity will end, it will disappear. I do not have to argue about that. I am certain! Jesus WAS OKAY, but His subjects were too simple, and today we are more famous than Jesus." (John Lennon, 1966)

S oon after he made this statement, John Lennon disappeared—ended. I do not have to argue about that. I am certain. He was shot to death by six bullets.

Nietzsche said, "God is dead." But God said, "Nietzsche is dead."

One of the most devastating realities today is that the bulk of humanity disrespects, demeans, and undervalues the God of all Creation. They joke about Him, curse Him, and disregard Him. They make themselves gods of their own lives and act as if they truly knew He didn't exist. But there is no one who deep down doesn't believe in God. Paul tells us this in Romans 1:18-19,

[18] For the wrath of God is revealed from Heaven against all ungodliness and unrighteousness of men, who suppress the truth in unrighteousness, [19] because what may be known of God is manifest in them, for God has shown *it* to them.

What can be known about God is "Plain to them." He explains that though "God has shown it to them," they are busy creating idols, which, along with God "Giving them over" in His wrath, causes them to live for their appetites and lusts. But what can be known about God is plain! Therefore, the problem is evasion. The deceitful human heart wants to look away from the Truth, from God. There is something there that it fears beyond all things.

But this is the great lie of Satan. That seeing God for Who He is would be our death and destruction. It's a lie. Seeing God for Who He is, is our salvation. Only when we see God rightly can we see ourselves rightly, see our condition, see and crave the true remedy, the cross of Christ, the blood of Jesus, and the adoption as Sons to this Great Father in Heaven we've tried so desperately *not* to see. Only then can we be set free to live and love in His light as we were created to do. So, Who is God? Let's not look away. Let's go into the throne room of all that is good and holy, and let's look, no matter the cost, because God is calling us to see and stop hiding with Adam in the woods behind our shame and fig leaves. Let's come out of our hiding place and see Him and let Him see us.

I want to begin this book where all things start (and end): with God. We must grapple with six truths about God before looking at man through a new lens. These six things are:

1. The Infinite Existence of God
2. The Omnipresence of God
3. The Omnipotence of God
4. The Triune Existence of God

5. The Holiness of God
6. The Infinite Love of God

These six things and their derivative attributes add up to "the Glory of God." The most potent exercise we can undertake is to stretch our minds as far as they can possibly be extended to comprehend the incomprehensible. We can never fully grasp the fullness of Who God is, but it is imperative to try according to what has been revealed. In the trying is our only hope of the blessing of "Marveling" at what is marvelous (2 Thes 1:10) and "Fearing God more than most men." (Neh 7:2) We will contemplate each attribute to come to the best possible understanding of Who God is. By God's grace, we will be left in awe, which is the proper human condition rarely truly experienced by sinful man.

The Infinite Existence of God

"God is, was, and always will be." (Heb 13:8, Rev 1:8)

In the beginning...God. This is how God's Word begins. (Gen 1:1) There was a beginning of creation, and as I said in the introduction, there was something before creation. God was there, always, and infinitely.

God and Time

Time is something altogether different from how we experience it. Einstein wrote of the "Space/time continuum:"

According to Space.com,

> Albert Einstein, in his theory of special relativity, determined that the laws of physics are the same for all non-accelerating observers, and he showed that the speed of light within a

vacuum is the same no matter the speed at which an observer travels, according to *Wired*.

As a result, he found that space and time were interwoven into a single continuum known as space-time. And events that occur at the same time for one observer could occur at different times for another.

According to special relativity, time is understood to be *relative* and can dilate or contract depending on the observer's motion. Einstein understood that an observer in motion relative to a stationary observer will experience time more slowly. This phenomenon has been experimentally confirmed in various ways, such as with high-speed particle accelerators.

Consider our microscopic Earth, sun, solar system, and galaxy and the proportions of these to the Infinite One. We can start to draw a picture of the relevance of what *time on our Earth is to God.* In other words, if time is relative between two moving observers, think of how comparable it is between man and God for Whom, "A day is as a thousand years, and a thousand years is as a day." (2 Pt 3:8)

Let us assume that inside the Being of God here is our tiny sun likened to an ultra-small bacterium and then try to comprehend a planet (Earth) spinning around that bacterium and that 8 billion gogglywidgets are living on that tiny planet with its sun (the bacterium) rising and setting on each of its *relative* days one day at a time.

If, in the blink of an eye, that bacterium (galaxy with its solar systems) dies and falls off the body as dust, this would not affect the God of Timelessness.

God is outside of time, and His day does not consist as our days do of our sun rising and setting each 24 hours. It all has no impact on Him.

"But do not overlook this one fact, beloved, that with the Lord one day is as a thousand years, and a thousand years as one day." (2 Pt 3:8) Peter could have said, "One day is as a trillion years."

In the entire universe, there is only one place that has a twenty-four-hour day, a seven-day week, and a 365-day year, and that is on planet Earth. 2 Timothy 1:9 speaks of God, "Who has saved us and called us with a holy calling, not according to our works, but according to His own purpose and grace which was given to us in Christ Jesus **before time began.**" "In hope of **eternal** life which God, Who cannot lie, promised **before time began.**" (Tit 1:2) Paul here is telling us that God put this in place before our world and our solar system. Then, *with material creation, time was brought into existence.*

"And this is eternal life, that they may know You, the only true God, and Jesus Christ Whom You have sent." (Jn 17:3)

I would like to pose the following questions concerning the fact that God exists outside of time:

1. Before our universe came into actualization/completion was there such a thing as time?

2. When God creates the new Heaven and Earth, will there be such a thing as time, or will it simply vanish away?

We humans are conditioned by the concept and experience of time with our watches, schedules, appointments, dates, calendars, time slots, etc. But I learned a long *time* back that giving the world twenty-four hours a day will want to take twenty-five plus. That is why John has told us,

[14] I have written to you, fathers, because you have known Him *Who is* from the beginning. I have written to you, young men, because you

are strong, and the Word of God abides in you, and you have overcome the wicked one.

[15] Do not love the world or the things in the world. If anyone loves the world, the love of the Father is not in him. [16] For all that *is* in the world—the lust of the flesh, the lust of the eyes, and the pride of life—is not of the Father but is of the world. [17] And the world is passing away, and the lust of it; but he who does the will of God abides forever. (1 Jn 2:14-17)

If we would have "the love of the Father" in us, we must expel the world's love, this time-bound prison (a prison because it is fallen). Indeed, we can only remove the love of the world *by* loving the Father–the Infinite One.

INFINITE

We live in one dimension, but in relatively recent history, scientists have discovered up to eight others: X-rays, gamma rays, microwaves, infrared rays, ultraviolet rays, radio waves, sun rays, and light rays. How many are still to be discovered? How many frequencies are there floating around in creation that we cannot see, touch, or perceive by our limited senses?

Just think of your radio, television, or computer, and every other technological gadget we have. How many waves and rays are in every room, home, car, or building?

God measures the universe, with its billions of galaxies, with the span of His hand. Isaiah 40:12 says: "Who has measured the waters in the hollow of His hand, measured Heaven with a span and calculated the dust of the Earth in a measure? Weighed the mountains in scales and the hills in a balance?"

He has to humble Himself to look upon His creation. He must *condescend* to "make the Earth His footstool." (Isa 66:1) Think of the incredible shrinking He must achieve.

Psalm 113:4-6 tells us that:

> [4] The LORD is high above all nations, and His glory above the heavens! [5] Who is like the LORD our God, Who is seated on high, [6] Who looks far down on the heavens and the Earth?

Verse 6 is better translated: "Who humbles Himself to behold the things that are in the heavens and in the Earth?"

It is a problem for the finite mind to comprehend infinity and an Infinite Being. We can only begin to grasp it by revelation. We experience time as not relative, but we know it is relative. In the same way, we experience God as existing in time with us since He *condescends* to do so, *but we know He is not bound by time, which is His creation.* We cannot fully comprehend, but we can and should be in awe. It bears stating that this is why we find it so hard to wait for Christ's return, but we'd be blessed to submit to His good plan and remember the words already stated by Peter: "That with the Lord one day *is* as a thousand years, and a thousand years as one day."

While it is not philosophically possible to fully grasp the infinite (which is only able to be grasped by revelation), what we do understand is "greatness" and the concept of "big," a word that can only serve as an understatement when thinking of the "bigness" of God. Perhaps one way to do it would be to look at smallness. Genesis 2:7 says: "And the Lord God formed man of the dust of the ground, and breathed into his nostrils the breath of life, and man became a living being."

Contemplate this and see where God takes you in your thinking. God took a pile of dust, added 30 trillion *cells,* plus some fluids He added later, and there stands a living, breathing soul, an embodied spirit, a human being. God spoke; He said, "Man, *live!*"

It's amusing to see how the evolutionists explain this one. How do they think these cells organized themselves into the intricate woven fabric of a human soul? Who decides who will become the eye, ear, foot, hand, spleen, or any other part?

Wikipedia tells us:

> There are about 30 trillion (3×10^{13}) human cells in the adult human body, varying from about 20 to 40 trillion depending on the sex, age, and weight, and a roughly equal number of bacterial cells.[1][2][3][4][5][6] The human cells have been categorized into over 400 cell types[2] based on location and function within the body, of which about 230 types are listed here.

Well, we can see that is not the answer. It certainly tells us what there is, but how it got here and turned into your aunt, we do not yet know. Perhaps *Britannica* can enlighten us:

What is a cell?
What is cell theory?
What do cell membranes do?

A cell, in biology, is the basic membrane-bound unit that contains the fundamental molecules of life and of which all living things are composed. A single cell is often a complete organism, such as a bacterium or yeast. Other cells acquire specialized functions as they mature. These cells cooperate with other specialized cells and become the building blocks of large multicellular organisms, such as humans and other animals. Although cells are much larger than atoms, they are still minimal. The smallest known cells are a group of tiny bacteria called mycoplasmas; some of these single-celled organisms are spheres as small as 0.2 μm in diameter (1μm = about 0.000039 inch), with a total mass of 10^{-14} grams—equal to that of 8,000,000,000 hydrogen atoms. Cells of humans typically have a mass 400,000 times larger than the mass of a single mycoplasma bacterium, but even human cells are only about 20 μm across. It would require a sheet of about 10,000 human cells to cover the head of a pin, and each human organism is composed of more than 30,000,000,000,000 cells.

Each one of these cells is like a small factory with its living working parts. Yes, we understand that, and it is amazing. Well done, science, for figuring that out. However, you have failed to answer our question. Who made it, and how did it get here—not to mention, how do these cells form whole body parts, let alone entire bodies?

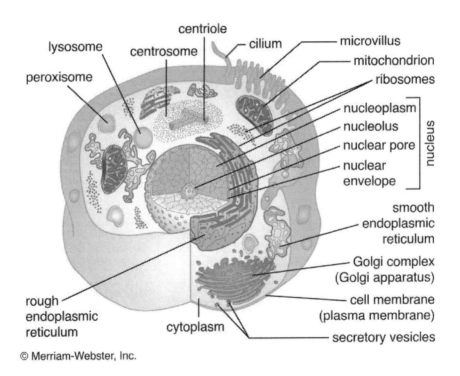

© Merriam-Webster, Inc.

Life on Earth

Perhaps a better way to approach this would be to ask how life in the universe came about from a scientific perspective. As of this writing, A.I. has become a relatively good aggregate resource for compiling the ultimate opinions of the almighty internet. Let us ask Chat GPT how life was formed. I'll also tell it to be succinct because Jesus is returning soon, and we don't have all day!

"How did carbon life form in the universe?"

> Chat GPT: The origin of carbon-based life in the universe is a complex and fascinating topic. ***While we don't have a definitive answer***, scientists have developed ***theories*** based on our understanding of astrophysics, chemistry, and biology.
>
> Here's a general overview:
>
> **Nucleosynthesis in Stars:**
> - Carbon and other elements essential for life are formed through nucleosynthesis in stars. Stellar fusion processes, particularly in the later stages of a star's life, involve synthesizing heavier elements from lighter ones.
> - In the core of stars, hydrogen atoms undergo fusion to form helium, releasing energy. As the star evolves, it can undergo additional fusion reactions, producing elements like carbon, oxygen, and nitrogen.
>
> **Supernova Explosions:**
> - The life cycle of a massive star culminates in a supernova explosion. During this explosive event, tremendous amounts of energy are released, and this process **can generate even heavier elements, including those necessary for life.**

- The debris from supernova explosions contains a mix of elements scattered into space. These materials form the raw building blocks for new stars, planets, and, **potentially, life.**

Formation of Planetary Systems:

- As the remnants of a supernova disperse, they can mix with other interstellar material and form a new generation of stars and planetary systems.
- Planets, including Earth, form from the leftover material in protoplanetary disks around young stars. These planets inherit the elements synthesized in previous stellar generations, including carbon.

Chemical Processes on Planets:

- On Earth, it underwent further chemical processes once the planet formed. Water, organic compounds, and other **essential molecules are formed through chemical reactions** on the surface and the delivery of materials from space, such as comets and asteroids.

Emergence of Life:

- **The transition from simple organic molecules to living organisms is a complex and not yet fully understood process. It likely** involved a series of chemical reactions leading to the formation of self-replicating molecules, such as RNA or DNA.

It's important to note that the study of **abiogenesis, the origin of life from non-living matter, is an ongoing field of research.** While the processes leading to the formation of carbon-based life have been **theorized**, many **details remain uncertain**, and scientists continue to explore these questions through laboratory experiments, observations, and **theoretical models**.

In other words, they don't know. They don't know how carbon *life* is formed. They don't know how that carbon life, if it did form, was turned into complex beings. They don't know. They theorize and pretend there is an answer. But there is only one answer. The infinite and omnipresent and powerful Creator spoke it into being. Even if they somehow proved their theories someday, who created the first elements (apparently hydrogen)? Where did it come from? Where was it kept? The answer: Infinity. God.

A story goes like this: All the world's leading DNA experts and genetic engineers got together to put forth a challenge to God; this was that challenge: *that they could make a human body.*

They harnessed the world's best technology and equipment in the finest laboratory ever known to man and gathered the most fertile pile of dust available. Then, they were ready and approached God with the challenge.

God's response was simple: He said, "Go and get your own pile of dust."

Returning to the cell universe, spend as much time as you can contemplating and grasping as far as the finite mind is capable, and you will be at the doorway to the infinite. You may knock, but you may not go in.

The Omnipresence of God

God is everywhere, always. He is omnipresent. He encompasses the furthest reaches of our universe, which we now know contains 1 to 2 trillion galaxies. All of these are included in the "second heaven" (2 Cor 12:1-4), which is contained within the Being of God. I'll repeat it. **God is everywhere *in* the universe; He exists *outside* the universe, and the universe exists *within Him.***

If you think you can completely take that in, think again.

Right here, at that start, we are faced with a question: "How does a finite human being comprehend an infinite Spirit?" Everyone talks about infinity as though it were comprehensible, but have you ever stopped to think that the concept is beyond our comprehension? Time goes infinitely far back to…where? It goes infinitely far into the future…where? That we have a word for it, *infinity* does not mean that we could possibly grasp it. Yet, we understand that our God is the One Who is, was, and always will be. (Ps 90:2)

Start from the most minute particle that has been discovered and then go out and out and out to infinity. There is only God.

> Now, for the first time, scientists have captured images of ultra-small bacteria, putting to rest a decades-old debate over whether these minuscule creatures exist.
>
> Led by scientists from the US Department of Energy's Lawrence Berkeley National Laboratory and the University of California, Berkeley, the team has confirmed that these single-celled organisms have an average volume of 0.009 cubic microns. One micron is one-millionth of a meter, which means 150 of them could fit inside an *E. coli* cell. This is the most diminutive life form known to science, and they could be as small as life gets on Earth.

And yet the presence of God and Jesus is there in each of them, providing them with life. Now start with infinity and come back down and down and down to that smallest microscopic particle of all this creation, and it is all still within God. Because of His omnipresence, He is present in this most minute particle, existing in all His fullness.

The Mystery of the Third Heaven

I said above that universal space is the "second heaven." The first heaven is the atmosphere above us. But God has revealed to us a mystery that has been held close to His chest for thousands of years through the writings of our brother Paul, who it appears was hesitant to write it all down and share it. It is the existence and mystery of the "third heaven," a precious gift of revelation into the Being that is God. As an aside, Paul describes His own experience in the vision of the heavenly realm and the special revelation he received from our Lord in 2 Corinthians 12:1-4:

> [1] I must go on boasting. Though there is nothing to be gained by it, I will go on to visions and revelations of the Lord. [2] I know a man in Christ who fourteen years ago was **caught up to the third heaven**—whether in or out of the body I do not know, God knows. [3] And I know that this man was caught up into paradise—whether in or out of the body I do not know, God knows— [4] and he **heard things that cannot be told, which man may not utter**.

Clearly, Paul is reluctant to share his most profoundly intimate moment with Christ in this place called "the third heaven." But we are left with the question: What is the third heaven to which Paul was caught up?

These verses so captivated my spirit that I sought the Lord for months until this revelation of what happened to Paul came to me piece by piece; it would have been too much to digest and take in in one sitting/kneeling, and I believe God revealed it to me in small bites for my good. I discerned here:

"The first heaven is the atmosphere that surrounds our planet Earth."

"The second heaven is the universe that encapsulates our solar system."

"The third heaven is God, and where HE dwells WHO encapsulates the universe, this is the heavenly realm and all that that entails."

Comprehending the third heaven is somewhat like attempting to understand infinity or the Triune God (One God in Three Persons all at once). Paul is not the only one to describe the third heaven. Others have done so in detail, though they did not refer to it as the third heaven. Isaiah saw it:

> [1] In the year that King Uzziah died, I saw the Lord sitting on a throne, high and lifted, and the train of His *robe* filled the temple. [2] Above it stood seraphim; each one had six wings: with two he covered his face, with two he covered his feet, and with two he flew. [3] And one cried to another and said:
>
>> "Holy, holy, holy *is* the LORD of hosts;
>> The whole Earth *is* full of His glory!"
>
> [4] And the posts of the door were shaken by the voice of him who cried out, and the house was filled with smoke.
>
> [5] So I said:
>
>> "Woe *is* me, for I am undone!
>> Because I *am* a man of unclean lips,
>> And I dwell in the midst of a people of unclean lips;
>> For my eyes have seen the King,
>> The LORD of hosts." (Isa 6:1-5)

Ezekiel saw it too:

[22] The likeness of the firmament above the heads of the living creatures was like the color of an awesome crystal, stretched out over their heads. [23] And under the firmament their wings spread out straight, one toward another. Each one had two which covered one side, and each one had two which covered the other side of the body. [24] When they went, I heard the noise of their wings, like the noise of many waters, like the voice of the Almighty, a tumult like the noise of an army; and when they stood still, they let down their wings. [25] A voice came from above the firmament that was over their heads; whenever they stood, they let down their wings.

[26] And above the firmament over their heads was the likeness of a throne, in appearance like a sapphire stone; on the likeness of the throne was a likeness with the appearance of a man high above it. [27] Also from the appearance of His waist and upward I saw, as it were, the color of amber with the appearance of fire all around within it; and from the appearance of His waist and downward I saw, as it were, the appearance of fire with brightness all around. [28] Like the appearance of a rainbow in a cloud on a rainy day, so was the appearance of the brightness all around it. This was the appearance of the likeness of the glory of the Lord. So, when I saw it, I fell on my face, and I heard a voice of One speaking. (Ez 1:22-28)

And Daniel:

[9] "As I looked,
   thrones were placed,
      and the Ancient of Days took His seat.
   His clothing was white as snow,
      and the hair of His head like pure wool;
   His throne was fiery flames;
      its wheels were burning fire.

> [10] A stream of fire issued
>   and came out from before Him;
> a thousand thousands served Him,
>   and ten thousand times ten thousand stood before Him;
> the court sat in judgment,
>   and the books were opened. (Dan 7:9-10)

Among the New Testament figures, Stephen, the first martyr, saw it (Acts 7), Peter, possibly, saw it on the roof in Joppa (Acts 10), and John, of course, saw it. His Revelation tells us:

> [1] After this I looked, and behold, a door standing open in Heaven! And the first voice, which I had heard speaking to me like a trumpet, said, "Come up here, and I will show you what must take place after this." [2] At once I was in the Spirit, and behold, a throne stood in Heaven, with one seated on the throne. [3] And he who sat there had the appearance of jasper and carnelian, and around the throne was a rainbow that had the appearance of an emerald. [4] Around the throne were twenty-four thrones, and seated on the thrones were twenty-four elders, clothed in white garments, with golden crowns on their heads. [5] From the throne came flashes of lightning, and rumblings and peals of thunder, and before the throne were burning seven torches of fire, which are the seven spirits of God, [6] and before the throne, there was as it were a sea of glass, like crystal.
>
> And around the throne, on each side of the throne, are four living creatures, full of eyes in front and behind, [7] the first living creature like a lion, the second living creature like an ox, the third living creature with the face of a man, and the fourth living creature like an eagle in flight. [8] And the four living creatures, each of them with six wings, are full of eyes all around and within, and day and night they never cease to say,

"Holy, holy, holy, is the Lord God Almighty,
    Who was and is and is to come!"

[9] And whenever the living creatures give glory and honor and thanks to Him Who is seated on the throne, Who lives forever and ever, [10] the twenty-four elders fall before Him Who is seated on the throne and worship him Who lives forever and ever. They cast their crowns before the throne, saying,

[11] "Worthy are You, our Lord and God,
    to receive glory and honor and power,
for You created all things,
    and by Your will they existed and were created." (Rev 4)

The first and second heavens are all inside and contained within God. They are just a part of His Being and His omnipresence.

In short, God is incomprehensible for a human mind to grasp except for what He has chosen to reveal. God's magnitude is beyond the scope of our ability to conceptualize. And yet, throughout the centuries, man has tried to make images to reflect God, or even worse, to say that these images *are* Gods. Even after the glorious rescue of the Israelites from slavery, they fell into this dark pit of confusion and folly.

[1] Now when the people saw that Moses delayed coming down from the mountain, the people gathered to Aaron, and said to him, "Come, make us Gods that shall go before us; for *as for* this Moses, the man who brought us up out of the land of Egypt, we do not know what has become of him."

[2] And Aaron said to them, "Break off the golden earrings which *are* in the ears of your wives, your Sons, and your daughters, and bring *them* to me." [3] So all the people broke off the golden earrings which *were* in their ears and brought *them* to Aaron. [4]

> And he received *the gold* from their hand, and he fashioned it with an engraving tool, and made a molded calf.
>
> Then they said, "This *is* your God, O Israel, that brought you out of the land of Egypt!" (Ex 32:1-4)

In our small, self-centered world, we are imprisoned by our lack of understanding. Many of us not only do not know what exists outside ourselves and our world, but we do not want to know. That something exists greater than us is threatening to many people.

Our societies are growing more insular every day, hiding in their caves of social media and internet propaganda. We don't even understand our next-door neighbors, let alone our neighboring countries. How much less is our planet and its atmosphere, universe, and the dimension outside our universe?

Psalm 2:1-12 says:

> [1] Why do the nations rage, and the people plot a vain thing?
>
> [2] The kings of the Earth set themselves,
>   and the rulers take counsel together,
>   against the LORD and against His Anointed, saying,
>
> [3] "Let us break their bonds in pieces
>   and cast away their cords from us."
>
> [4] He who sits in the heavens shall laugh;
>   the Lord shall hold them in derision.
>
> [5] Then He will speak to them in His wrath,
>   and distress them in His deep displeasure:
>
> [6] "Yet I have set My King
>   on My holy hill of Zion."

[7] I will declare the decree:
  The LORD has said to Me, "You are My Son;
  Today, I have begotten You.

[8] Ask of Me, and I will give You the nations for Your
  inheritance, and the ends of the Earth for Your possession.

[9] You shall break them with a rod of iron;
  You shall dash them to pieces like a potter's vessel."

[10] Now, therefore, be wise, O kings.
  Be instructed, you judges of the Earth.

[11] Serve the LORD with fear,
  and rejoice with trembling.

[12] Kiss the Son, lest He be angry, and you perish in the way,
  when His wrath is kindled but a little.
  Blessed are all those who put their trust in Him.

To know God is to know the omnipresence of God, a fact that can be accepted, while not fully understood. We should do our best, but at the end of the finiteness of our minds, we should say, "Who can understand these things?" (1 Cor 2:14)

The Omnipotence of God

We have discussed in detail the barely comprehensible omnipresence of God. But it is also crucial to understand what can be comprehended about the *omnipotence of God*. While the omnipresence of God means that He is everywhere always, the omnipotence of all means that *He is all-powerful*. That is such a brief and succinct way to understate this reality. When we think of "All-powerful," we think of a dictator of a mighty nation. The dictator is not all-powerful. He is a vapor, a breath that will soon wither away like grass. (Ps 37:2) God is the true meaning of all-encompassing power: omnipotence.

There is nothing that God cannot accomplish that is good to complete. You know of nothing else and no one that is all-powerful, so before we think we understand the meaning of the concept, humility would beg us to stop and reconsider.

The Power Behind All Powers

Where does all life on Earth come from? Is it not from our sun? 1,300,000 planet Earths can fit inside of the sun. All light, all energy, and all life on Earth depend on our sun. If the energy coming from the sun is responsible for all the life we know of, then consider how much *power* is generated from just this star. The power of one sun is incredible and *would seem* limitless in its ability to generate energy.

Astronomers gauge that there are up to 2 trillion galaxies in our universe. The same experts say that there are between 100 billion and 400 billion stars in our galaxy alone, and our galaxy is 100,000 light-years across (a light year is the distance something travels at the incredible speed of light to travel in one earthly year). But it is small compared to our neighboring galaxy, Andromeda, which is 220,000 light-years across and 2.2 times the size of our galaxy.

If you do not grasp the finite's vastness, go back and read the last two paragraphs. We cannot hope to grasp the infinite if we do not grasp the finite.

Now consider: Where does our one little sun get its power and energy from? God alone provides it. **All stars draw their life and energy from God and His only begotten Son, Jesus Christ.**

One human eye has over 100 million rod cells with over 2 million working parts. Meditate on this for a while and think of our sun *as just one minute cell* in God's Being. I assure you, that is being generous toward the sun. Then compare our galaxy to one flake of dandruff on the head of God—*more than generous.* Let's *start* to see God through this filter and the magnitude of comparison considering what we have already looked at, and we can take this as an overly exaggerated version of proportion in our human favor.

Sit back and reflect on this: If this tiny flake of dandruff (our galaxy) were to fall to the ground from the head of God, that would be of absolutely no moment to Him. It would make not one scrap of difference to His Being whatsoever. Yet, He, the Father, has such immeasurable love for His creation that He sent His amazing, beautiful Son to us so that we could see Him and that He could display His love and Person *for us to develop the most profound and significant relationship with Him.* He has *condescended* to make "the Earth His footstool." (Isa 66:1) Can you grasp the degree to which God has to shrink Himself to make the Earth His footstool?

With modern science and technology, we understand the power of our sun and its effect on our planet. We also know how awesome in power it is compared to each of us, individual molecules of life buzzing around our globe, thinking the world and the universe revolve around us.

We need to be jolted by a wake-up call to come to terms with the actual dimensions and proportions between us and the magnitude and the power of the omnipotent self-existing God.

Man needs to stop thinking of himself in the following three ways: First, there is the naive belief that the universe revolves around and exists for the sole purpose of our solar system. Then there are those less intelligent who believe that everything exists and revolves around our Earth. Finally, we reach the rock bottom of depravity with those who believe everything exists and revolves around themselves.

Jesus told us in Matthew 16:26: "For what profit is it to a man if he gains the whole world, and loses His own soul? Or what will a man give in exchange for His soul?"

What He is telling us is if any man or woman pursues this microscopic piece of galactic dust and rejects the only true God and Jesus Christ, Whom He sent with all that He offers, eternal life with Him, and sharing all that He is and has with His children, they would have to be an utter fool. But even worse, they would have to be utterly blind. Oh, God, use me to tear the scales off the eyes of a lost generation! God is all-powerful; He is omnipotent, and what He deserves is nothing less than our abject worship.

The Triune Existence of God

We describe nothing in this chapter that the natural mind can truly comprehend. We cannot understand God's infinite nature and existence, the self-existence of God, and we cannot understand the Trinity. That is, we were created and sustained by one God Who is in Three Persons: God the Father, God the Son, and God the Holy Spirit. This section will not be a complete treatise on the Trinity, which would require volumes, but I hope it will be enough to increase the reader's awe of the truth.

God the Son: Jesus Christ

We have been considering God, and in that, primarily the Being and Person of God the Father, to Whom Christ, the Son of God, was in very nature and also prayed to and obeyed: "Yet not my will, but yours be done."

Now, we must look briefly at the incomparable Person that is Jesus. This Son Who will "Rule the nations with a rod of iron" (Rev 2:27) and Who will be acknowledged and loved as He rightfully deserves on that great day when "Every knee shall bow, and every tongue shall confess" that He is King of kings and Lord of lords Who shall reign forever and ever. John 1:1-5, 9-11 (CJB) says:

> [1] In the beginning was the Word, and the Word was with God, and the Word was God.
>
> [2] He was in the beginning with God.
>
> [3] All things were made through Him, and without Him nothing was made that was made.
>
> [4] In Him was life, and the life was the light of men.
>
> [5] And the light shines in the darkness, and the darkness did not comprehend it.
>
> [9] That was the true light, which gives light to every man coming into the world.
>
> [10] He was in the world, and the world was made through Him, and the world did not know Him.
>
> [11] He came to His own, and His own did not receive Him.

Then verses 14 and 18 tell us:

> [14] And the Word became flesh and dwelled among us, and we beheld His glory, the glory as of the only begotten of the Father, full of grace and truth.

> [18] No one has seen God at any time. The only begotten Son, Who is in the bosom of the Father, He has declared Him.

Colossians 1:15-17 says:

> [15] He is the image of the invisible God, the firstborn over all creation, [16] for by Him all things were created that are in Heaven and that are on Earth, visible and invisible, whether thrones or dominions or principalities or powers. All things were created through Him and for Him. [17] And He is before all things, and in Him all things consist.

Verse 19-20:

> [19] For it pleased the Father that in Him all the fullness should dwell, [20] and by Him to reconcile all things to Himself, by Him, whether things on Earth or things in Heaven, having made peace through the blood of His cross.

Jesus is the Word, the Logos, the logic and meaning behind all creation. He is the reason all creation exists and the meaning behind everything. For example, Astrology (astro-logos), Biology, Meteorology, and Zoology—Jesus is the answer to everything.

One of Jesus's many incredible statements about Himself was that He is *the Life*. We can only surmise one thing from that: everything that has life draws its life from Him. Every galaxy, every star, every planet exists because of Him, and every insect, plant, animal, and sea creature all owe their lives and existence to Him. Jesus, God's Son, is in very nature God and has existed for all time in perfect harmony with God, in staggering infinity, and He was not only there at creation, but He was the Word by which the creation came into being.

Jesus, one day, will discard this universe. Simply like removing a shirt, He will fold it (the universe) up and put it away. Then Jesus will take out a new one and clothe Himself with that.

Hebrews 1:8-12 says:

> [8] But to the Son He says:
>
> "Your throne, O God, is forever and ever;
>   a scepter of righteousness is the scepter of Your kingdom.
>
> [9] You have loved righteousness and hated lawlessness;
>   therefore God, Your God, has anointed You
>   with the oil of gladness more than Your companions."
>
> [10] And, "You, Lord, in the beginning, laid the foundation of the
>   Earth, and the heavens are the work of Your hands.
>
> [11] They will perish, but You remain,
>   and they will all grow old like a garment;
>
> [12] Like a cloak, You will fold them up,
>   and they will be changed.
> But You are the same,
>   and Your years will not fail."

Psalm 102:25-27 says:

> [25] Of old You laid the foundation of the Earth,
>   and the heavens are the work of Your hands.
> [26] They will perish, but You will endure;
>   like a cloak, You will change them and they will be changed.
> [27] But You are the same, and Your years will have no end.

Psalm 139:1-16:

¹ O LORD, You have searched me and known me!

² You know my sitting down and my rising up;
   You understand my thought afar off.

³ You comprehend my path and my lying down,
   and are acquainted with all my ways.

⁴ For there is not a word on my tongue.
   But behold, O LORD, You know it altogether.

⁵ You have hedged me behind and before,

   and laid Your hand upon me.

⁶ Such knowledge is too wonderful for me.
   It is high; I cannot attain it.

⁷ Where can I go from Your Spirit?
   Or where shall I flee from Your presence?

⁸ If I ascend to Heaven, You are there;
   if I make my bed in Hell, You are there.

⁹ If I take the wings of the morning
   and dwell in the uttermost parts of the sea.

¹⁰ Even there, Your hand shall lead me,
   and Your right hand shall hold me.

¹¹ If I say, "Surely the darkness shall fall on me,"
   even the night shall be light about me.

¹² Indeed, the darkness shall not hide from You,
   but the night shines as the day;
   the darkness and the light are both alike to You.

¹³ For you formed my inward parts;
  You covered me in my mother's womb.

¹⁴ I praise You, for I am fearfully and wonderfully made.
  Marvelous are Your works,
  and that my soul knows very well.

¹⁵ My frame was not hidden from You,
  when I was made in secret,
  and skillfully wrought in the lowest parts of the Earth.

¹⁶ Your eyes saw my substance, being yet unformed.
  And in Your Book they all were written,
  the days fashioned for me,
  when as yet there were none of them.

What is incomprehensible, God, the Word has made comprehensible through revelation. Jesus has never left anybody in the dark. He told us *everything* we will ever need to know about His Father and the Holy Spirit. Imagine what it must have been like with a lesser revelation. I mean that God's people were still guessing on quite a lot until Christ. The prophets had heard clearly and spoken God's Word, but there was so much they did not know or understand. Consider that Jesus did not only *tell* us about the Father, He *showed* us the Father.

⁵ Thomas said to him, "Lord, we do not know where you are going. How can we know the way?" ⁶ Jesus said to him, "I am the way, and the truth, and the life. No one comes to the Father except through me. ⁷ **If you had known me, you would have known my Father also**. From now on you do know him and have seen him."

⁸ Philip said to him, "Lord, **show us the Father**, and it is enough for us." ⁹ Jesus said to him, "Have I been with you so long, and you still do not know me, Philip? **Whoever has seen**

me has seen the Father. How can you say, 'Show us the Father'? [10] Do you not believe that I am in the Father and the Father is in me? The words that I say to you I do not speak on my own authority, but **the Father Who dwells in me** does His works." (Jn 14:5-10 ESV Emphasis added)

Psalm 104 says:

> [1] Bless the LORD, O my soul!
>   O LORD my God, You are very great!
>   You are clothed with splendor and majesty,
>
> [2] covering Yourself with light as with a garment,
>   stretching out the heavens like a tent.
>
> [3] He lays the beams of His chambers on the waters;
>   He makes the clouds His chariot;
>   He rides on the wings of the wind;
>
> [4] He makes His messengers winds,
>   His ministers a flaming fire.
>
> [5] He set the Earth on its foundations,
>   so that it should never be moved.
>
> [6] You covered it with the deep as with a garment;
>   the waters stood above the mountains.
>
> [7] At Your rebuke they fled;
>   at the sound of Your thunder they took to flight.
>
> [8] The mountains rose, the valleys sank down
>   to the place that You appointed for them.
>
> [9] You set a boundary that they may not pass,
>   so that they might not again cover the Earth.

¹⁰ You make springs gush forth in the valleys;
    they flow between the hills;

¹¹ they give drink to every beast of the field;
    the wild donkeys quench their thirst.

¹² Beside them the birds of the heavens dwell;
    they sing among the branches.

¹³ From Your lofty abode You water the mountains;
    the Earth is satisfied with the fruit of Your work.

¹⁴ You cause the grass to grow for the livestock
    and plants for man to cultivate,
    that he may bring forth food from the Earth,

¹⁵ and wine to gladden the heart of man,
    oil to make his face shine
    and bread to strengthen man's heart.

¹⁶ The trees of the LORD are watered abundantly,
    the cedars of Lebanon that He planted.

¹⁷ In them the birds build their nests;
    the stork has her home in the fir trees.

¹⁸ The high mountains are for the wild goats;
    the rocks are a refuge for the rock badgers.

¹⁹ He made the moon to mark the seasons;
    the sun knows it's time for setting.

²⁰ You make darkness, and it is night,
    when all the beasts of the forest creep about.

²¹ The young lions roar for their prey,
    seeking their food from God.

[22] When the sun rises, they steal away
    and lie down in their dens.

[23] Man goes out to his work
    and to his labor until the evening.

[24] O LORD, how manifold are your works!
    In wisdom have You made them all;
    the Earth is full of Your creatures.

[25] Here is the sea, great and wide,
    which teems with creatures innumerable,
    living things both small and great.

[26] There go the ships,
    and Leviathan, which You formed to play in it.

[27] These all look to You,
    to give them their food in due season.

[28] When You give it to them, they gather it up;
    when You open your hand, they are filled with good
    things.

[29] When You hide Your face, they are dismayed;
    when You take away their breath, they die
    and return to their dust.

[30] When you send forth Your Spirit, they are created,
    and You renew the face of the ground.

[31] May the glory of the LORD endure forever;
    may the LORD rejoice in His works,

[32] Who looks on the Earth and it trembles,
    Who touches the mountains and they smoke!

³³ I will sing to the LORD as long as I live;
  I will sing praise to my God while I have being.

³⁴ May my meditation be pleasing to Him,
  for I rejoice in the LORD.

³⁵ Let sinners be consumed from the Earth,
  and let the wicked be no more!
  Bless the LORD, O my soul!
  Praise the LORD!

Jesus is the aroma of life. In John 3, Nicodemus came to Jesus by night and said to Him "You are different from us, there is no One like You". John 3:2 says:

> This man came to Jesus by night and said to Him, "Rabbi, we know that You are a teacher come from God; for no one can do these signs that You do unless God is with him."

Nicodemus was a Pharisee. These people were the leading church leaders of the day. Nicodemus could see that he and his peers didn't measure up to the standards of God and was humble enough to admit that and come to Jesus for guidance.

What was this display of humility saying? These Pharisees meticulously went about pretending religion; they had the temple and were carrying out the sacrifices, having everything in its correct position and place, and putting on an excellent show. Times have not changed, and neither has the human love for religion.

Nicodemus was saying, "We, the church leaders, are hypocrites; we have painted the outside to make it all look very respectful, pious, and holy, and as though we are the only contact with GOD." However, in reality, they were just like everybody else with sin dwelling inside of them, spiritually tearing themselves apart.

The people looked at them and were honest with themselves, saying "If these white-walled sepulchers with dead men's bones on the inside playing their hypocritical games cannot fulfill God's laws, then what hope is there for us mere souls." This play-acting created a stench of death surrounding all that their religion did, because the people could see righteousness in this life was unobtainable. What did they do? They simply gave up and went about living their daily lives. This has not changed, and today, people see straight through the hypocrisy and play-acting with those running and attending churches, getting their eternal life insurance policies stamped each week. The "Pharisees" of today are the same as themselves throughout their lives all week???

I want to avoid making a blanket statement here. There are countless amazing, wonderful brothers and sisters worldwide who are laying down their lives for Christ daily, and then when I stop and consider my own walk in comparison, I would like to shrink away onto my knees. But I do not believe they are the norm.

Religion took on a new face and everything changed when the Christ, the Savior of our fallen world, came onto the scene. People could immediately smell the sweet aroma of life because the life was dwelling bodily with them. And more than this, what they could see and smell for the first time in their lives was this ability to fulfill every law of God in a human life.

Jesus made this statement about Himself, "Who can find fault in Me?" And when He posed this question, not one person could reply in the negative to His claim. Jesus Christ is perfect, offering us His perfection and righteousness. We cannot come to God with our self-righteousness; it is utterly offensive to Him because it is entangled with so much *un*righteousness.

Our Own Righteousness

Our righteousness is as "filthy rags." (Isa) Paul tells us our self-righteousness is like human feces and a stench in God's nostrils. When we first come to Jesus, we need to come warts and all with a heart of repentance, wanting Him to change our lives. We want them to be fashioned into the life that we see in Him; He will then give us piece by piece His perfection and His righteousness.

> [21] But now the righteousness of God apart from the law is revealed, being witnessed by the law and the prophets, [22] Even the righteousness of God, through faith in Jesus Christ, to all and on all who believe. (Ro 3:21-22a)

We come as children, then we grow and learn obedience, bringing the depth and closeness of a relationship that gets sweeter and purer by the day. We so desperately need this righteousness as we so desperately need His love in us.

RELIGION IS EXTERNAL; RELATIONSHIP IS INTERNAL DISPLAYED FROM THE INSIDE OUT.

And only Christ can achieve it in us. I will write further on this later in the chapter. For now, there is one huge difference between Jesus Christ and every other human being, including Mohammed, Buddha, Confucius, and every prophet, priest, ruler, dictator, emperor, or king.

Jesus made each one of them. Now, He sits at the right hand of His Father in Heaven and intercedes for us. He is with us through His Holy Spirit.

The Holy Spirit

I have written more extensively (in a later chapter) on God, the Holy Spirit, but for now, understand that from start to finish, the Bible details the work of the Holy Spirit, starting with Genesis 1:2: "The Earth was without form, and void; and darkness *was* on the face of the deep. And the Spirit of God was hovering over the face of the waters." But His real prominence begins with Acts 2 when not only the promise of Jesus to send a Helper is fulfilled, but also the very prophecy of Joel.

²⁸ "And it shall come to pass afterward
that I will pour out My Spirit on all flesh;
Your sons and your daughters shall prophesy,
Your old men shall dream dreams,
Your young men shall see visions.

²⁹ And also on *My* menservants and on *My* maidservants
I will pour out My Spirit in those days."

³⁰ "And I will show wonders in the heavens and in the Earth,
blood and fire and pillars of smoke.

³¹ The sun shall be turned into darkness,
and the moon into blood, before the coming of the great and
awesome Day of the LORD.

³² And it shall come to pass,
that whoever calls on the name of the LORD
shall be saved.

For in Mount Zion and in Jerusalem, there shall be
deliverance, as the LORD has said,
among the remnant whom the LORD calls."
(Joel 2:28-32)

Since the Day of Pentecost, the Holy Spirit has been available to each Christian to the extent that they agree to "Be filled." The Holy Spirit is the quintessential Gentleman Who is preparing the bride/the Church for the great wedding day in which she is to become one with the bridegroom/Jesus Christ. He will never force Himself upon any of us, and He will never take away a person's freewill.

What Jesus said about Him and the honor He bestowed upon Him is matchless. He also provides us with the gravest of warnings to never, ever try to attribute the gifts of the Holy Spirit as coming from the adversary. I have endeavored to witness to people who have committed this unpardonable sin: They have made comments to me such as, "Speaking in tongues is of the devil." My endeavor to convert them to Christ was a complete waste of time; they had dug their own grave with their mouths.

Mark 3:28-30 says:

> [28] "Assuredly, I say to you, all sins will be forgiven the sons of men, and whatever blasphemies they may utter; [29] but, he who blasphemes against the Holy Spirit never has forgiveness, but is subject to eternal condemnation"— [30] because they said, "He has an unclean spirit."

In Luke 3:22, we learn that God the Son, Who in some mysterious way laid down an aspect of His divinity to Incarnate on the Earth, went about in His ministry manifesting God by the power of the Holy Spirit given to Him at His baptism. It says: "And the Holy Spirit descended in bodily form like a dove upon Him, and a voice came from Heaven which said, 'You are My beloved Son; in You, I am well pleased.'"

Jesus did not perform one miracle; He healed no one, nor did He preach one sermon until the Holy Spirit empowered him. It is then foolish for any one of us to believe that we could accomplish any of the works Jesus did without Him, the Holy Spirit.

I love reading those first few verses in our Bibles that so richly describe how the Holy Trinity created everything, bringing them together into their beings. (Gen 1:2-3) **The Father spoke the Word–Jesus Christ– with the Holy Spirit brooding over all creation as they orchestrated in flawless harmony, bringing every cell and atom together perfectly.**

Consider the latest discoveries we know and understand because we have reached out into outer space and plumbed the depths of the oceans with all these fantastic living creatures previously unknown. What is still left to be discovered? What is hidden from the naked eye? It boggles the mind.

Gifts of the Spirit

One function of God the Spirit is to give spiritual gifts to God's people. There is no Christian who has not been assigned at least one. All the gifts listed throughout Scripture are the gifts of the Holy Spirit. (Ro 12:6-8, 1 Cor 12:8-10)

Romans 12:6-8 says:

> [6] Having then gifts differing according to the grace that is given to us, *let us use them:* if prophecy, *let us prophesy* in proportion to our faith; [7] or ministry, *let us use it* in *our* ministering; he who teaches, in teaching; [8] he who exhorts, in exhortation; he who gives, with liberality; he who leads, with diligence; he who shows mercy, with cheerfulness.

1 Corinthians 12:8-10 tells us:

> [8] For to one is given the word of wisdom through the Spirit, to another the word of knowledge through the same Spirit, [9] to another faith by the same Spirit, to another gifts of healings by the same Spirit, [10] to another the working of miracles, to another prophecy, to another discerning of spirits, to another *different* kinds of tongues, to another the interpretation of tongues.

Each of us is given at least one of these gifts, because no one is entirely like Christ, Who bears them all. God intended that the Church would be like a body, and the only way to fully embody Christ's nature is to be together, combining our gifts and talents and empowered by One Spirit. When the Church refuses to operate in the fullness of our spiritual gifts, we fail to live up to the potential given to us by God.

The Fruit of the Spirit

All nine flavors of the fruit of life are the fruits of the Holy Spirit. Paul lists them in Galatians 5:22: "But the fruit of the Spirit is love, joy, peace, longsuffering, kindness, goodness, faithfulness, gentleness, self-control. Against such there is no law."

Who or what Christian would want to have any of these 16 gifts or these nine flavors of the one fruit missing as part of their relationship and walk with their God, the Holy Spirit?

Paul tells us here that we need to resolutely intently pursue the gifts from the Holy Spirit.

Grab them like a child at Christmas when opening her presents, wanting to investigate and use these wonderful new gifts. His gifts are the most addictive thing in a submitted human soul's life; once you have opened one, you will be champing at the bit and leaning into the harness to open and try the next, and the next, and so on.

Love: When desiring spiritual gifts, there remains one word of caution. No spiritual gift is more important than love. 1 Corinthians 12:31 says: "But earnestly desire the best gifts. And yet I show you a more excellent way." What is the more excellent way? To answer this question, read through the great love chapter, 1 Corinthians 13 through 14:1, which aptly describes this "More excellent way." "Pursue love, and desire spiritual gifts, but especially that you may prophesy." (1 Cor 14:1)

It is the combination of the selfless *agape* love of Jesus with the gifts of the Holy Spirit working together in unison *as They did at the beginning of creation.*

God the Holy Spirit will keep lifting Jesus up in your life and will faithfully teach you to make Him Lord of your life, day by day, as you listen to Him and then obey what you hear from Him.

I will go into much greater detail about this in a later chapter but know that being filled with the Holy Spirit is not optional. He is not a genie in a bottle; He is the Lord of our life and is meant to live in us.

The Holiness of God

One of God's most important and awe-inspiring characteristics, one that sets Him utterly apart from His created beings, is His Holiness. This renders Him worthy of complete devotion as One perfect in goodness and righteousness. God is perfect and set apart. To be holy is to be unapproachable. Scripture is full of proof that the Holiness of God would devour the sinner who approaches apart from the cleansing grace of God. When Isaiah met the Lord face to face, didn't he believe himself to be a dead man because of His "uncleanness?" (Isa 6:4)

Didn't the seraphim have to come with the fiery coal of God's cleansing furnace to make him able to stand? Didn't the High Priest have to undergo the ritual cleansing to the exact specifications which were by the grace of God to enter the Holy of Holy places? God is high and lifted–set apart. He is wholly "Other."

God's character is unquestionable finality, *absolute*, without reservations or conditions; certain, not to be doubted, total. As One Who is holy, He is pure. What comes to our world in the grip of evil, and it can't and doesn't want to let go? It is reciprocated both ways. We love the evil as much as it loves having us under its control; both sides are insatiable. This would have been unimaginable even just 30 years ago, but we are passing the point of no return.

Another way to say God is Holy is to say He is *perfect*. In an imperfect world, how do we understand perfection? It can only come one way, and that is, to look at Jesus, the only perfect man Who has ever lived. There was no question He could not answer, and no one man could provide an adequate response for every question He asked. In every world situation that has ever come to pass, He gave us the solution to rectify its complexity, no matter how difficult the situation. In every broken life, body, heart, or relationship, Jesus provided the solution if only we would apply His healing in our lives. He told us everything we need to know. Only our human failing gets in the way of the repair.

Consider the word *righteous*. The word means *perfectly* just, *perfectly* moral, in a *perfect* and right standing before the Holy One. Only God is righteous in Himself. There is no righteousness for humanity apart from the alien righteousness of Christ imputed to men. By righteousness, we can "Seek the Kingdom of God and His righteousness." Otherwise, there is "No one righteous, not even one" (Ro 3:8-10), no one but God.

What Have We Done?

Only one Being exists in Himself, sustains Himself, and relies only on Himself. All other life is utterly interdependent and ultimately dependent on Him to sustain. It is hard not to be negative when we look at what we have done to God and this beautiful, perfect planet He has given us. What have we done to this world that was created in perfection and called "Very good?" How have we taken what was holy and made it unholy?

I live on a farm in Australia where I fight daily with the non-native pests that kill our native vegetation. Without exception, every country on Earth suffers from the same problem of introduced species. This is analogous to what man has done to God's creation. Look at what he has introduced into our world and the destruction it is causing on a global scale. We are killing what this planet was created for, among other things, holiness.

If man has perfected one art, it is the art of unholy self-annihilation. Almost every significant scientific discovery has been mutated and used to kill. "War is the mother of invention."

God gives life; we bring death. God gives us beauty; we make things ugly. God gave us peace; we make war. God gave us perfection; we bring pollution, and so on. We can't help ourselves. Everything we touch, we corrupt. God is Holy; we are unholy (apart from Him).

The Beauty of Holiness and the Righteousness God displayed in His creation in every fantastic sunrise or sunset, the mountains and forests, the birth of a newborn babe, and every newborn animal cause us to sit in wonder and marvel at the perfection He gives us day after day. We now have a population of 8 billion people, and God produces enough food yearly to feed everyone on Earth. There is enough produce grown

WHO IS GOD AND WHO ARE WE?

every year to feed the animals we eat. That produce would feed the 8 billion people if fed to them. Our problem is not what God provides but how man distributes what He has provided us.

The Desperate Question

Every Christian needs to question themselves and their lives. They need to ask themselves, "What have I done for other people?" and "What am I doing for them now?" If we don't, one day Jesus will ask that question of every one of us. Ask it now. Don't wait. We say, "Oh, I'm doing this for my family," when we are really acting for our own benefit, for instance, when we neglect that very family to make more and more money.

The Infinite Love of God

The last trait we will explore is God's infinite love for us. The love with which the Father loves His children is *agape*. Agape is not the unconditional love now so widely preached and taught in the seeker-sensitive churches, which are all the rage. The "Nonjudgmental love of God" that people claim is in our Bibles is not there. People are evading the fact of God's justice and judgment. They don't want God to judge them.

There is a significant disparity between these two thoughts/theological outlooks. The first and biblical view is all about God and His sovereignty and everything that comes with that: His mercy, grace, and forgiveness freely given, wanting and expecting nothing back except relationship.

The second and unbiblical view is all about "me" and what God can do for me, forgiving every sin I ever commit without repercussions. Over 104 references in our New Testament relate directly to a believer losing their salvation through their negligence to sin. May this be sobering to us and drive us to the infinitely loving arms of our Father.

In His love, God gave everything to humankind, even His most precious Son, so that He could reveal Himself to us and so that we could know Him and enter an eternal relationship with Him. We must never take for granted what has been done for us nor cheapen the price paid to release us from our sins.

As quoted above, on the night before our Lord was crucified, Philip asked Him to show them, the 11 disciples/apostles, the Father. Jesus' response was, "I have been with you night and day for 3 1/2 years, and through ME you have seen and lived with the Father." (Jn 14:8)

Also, on this night, the night before His crucifixion, Jesus, knowing what was going to transpire the next day, spoke only of their welfare continually telling them, "Let not your hearts be troubled." (Jn 14:1) He said He must leave them, as was spoken of by the prophets. Still, He would send the Comforter, the Holy Spirit, to take His place.

Read John Chapters 13 through 17 to understand the selfless heart of Christ. Chapter 17, the real Lord's Prayer, reaches its peak in these passages with Jesus asking His Father, not once, but twice if He could please love us in the same way the Father loves Himself, Jesus. Then, the next day, as all the prophesied events unfolded according to Scripture, the Savior of the world displayed His selfless *agape* love again.

Firstly, He prayed, asking the Father to forgive those who were crucifying Him "for they did not know what they were doing." (Lk 23:34) Then Jesus, out of concern for His mother, asked the beloved disciple John to care for His mother now that He was going. (Jn 19:26) And even more astonishing than this, when the thief being crucified next to Him asked to be remembered when Jesus came into His

Kingdom, Jesus responded with these words: "Today you will be with Me in paradise." (Lk 23:43)

Most Christians have heard this so many times as to be numb to the outrageous nature of all this. But don't forget that it is all incomprehensible for humans to grasp. This was not just another human being but our God in action. This was *agape*–selfless love.

What an Amazing God we have!

1 Corinthians 13:4-14 (NKJV) tells us:

> [4] Love suffers long *and* is kind; love does not envy; love does not parade itself, is not puffed up; [5] does not behave rudely, does not seek its own, is not provoked, thinks no evil; [6] does not rejoice in iniquity, but rejoices in the truth; [7] bears all things, believes all things, hopes all things, endures all things.
>
> [8] Love never fails. But whether *there are* prophecies, they will fail; whether *there are* tongues, they will cease; whether *there is* knowledge, it will vanish away. [9] For we know in part, and we prophesy in part. [10] But when that which is perfect has come, then that which is in part will be done away.
>
> [13] When I was a child, I spoke as a child, I understood as a child, I thought as a child; but when I became a man, I put away childish things. [12] For now we see in a mirror, dimly, but then face to face. Now I know in part, but then I shall know just as I also am known.
>
> [13] And now abide faith, hope, love, these three; but the greatest of these *is* love.

Nothing Like Us

What we finite humans have completely missed in our humanity is that God is nothing like us. Because of the world we live in and our finite minds, we have, over the centuries, consumed the misconception from religion and its leaders that God is like us in all His forms. He is not—*not remotely.*

This has led humans to make images of gods that do not exist or are demonic pretenders, just manufactured by human hands. Idolatry extends beyond graven images. Even Christians have fallen for this in our desire to understand what cannot be understood.

We have been educated to think that the One True God Who made the universe is floating around inside of it somewhere and somehow controlling it like a manufactured machine, all because we are incapable of thinking outside of ourselves and our own little world—a world we have made in our own image.

Once, when the disciples were learning one of the most complicated doctrines of the faith, the doctrine of the Trinity, Jesus showed the Father by the Spirit who dwelled in Him, but they also saw that Jesus communicated with the Father. When the disciples came to Him after hearing how He spoke and shared with His Father, they asked Him, "How can we talk and communicate with God like You do?"

> [1] Now it came to pass, as He was praying in a certain place, when He ceased, *that* one of His disciples said to Him, "Lord, teach us to pray, as John also taught His disciples."
>
> [2] So He said to them, "When you pray, say:
>
> Our Father in Heaven,
> Hallowed be Your name.

Your kingdom come.
Your will be done
On Earth as *it is* in Heaven.

[3] Give us day by day our daily bread.

[4] And forgive us our sins,
For we also forgive everyone who is indebted to us.
And do not lead us into temptation,
But deliver us from the evil one." (Lk 11:1-4 NKJV)

Jesus' first words, "Our Father in Heaven," here in Luke 11, He is telling all of us in four short words the whereabouts and magnitude of God and that He is not like us human beings in finite bodies limited to five senses and confined to this Earth. In John 4, Jesus goes even further, telling us God is a Spirit and that we "Must worship Him in spirit and truth," for that is how He requires us to worship Him.

John 4:21-24 says:

[21] Jesus said to her, "Woman, believe Me, the hour is coming when you will neither on this mountain, nor in Jerusalem, worship the Father. [22] You worship what you do not know; we know what we worship, for salvation is of the Jews. [23] But the hour is coming, and now is, when the true worshipers will worship the Father in spirit and truth; for the Father is seeking such to worship Him. [24] God *is* Spirit, and those who worship Him must worship in spirit and truth."

When people wonder what is beyond our universe, they conclude that it is space, but then space has to have an end. We must take a humble seat and acknowledge that what is beyond our universe is God and His Heaven—the Creator Who is infinite and a Spirit. Isaiah 40:6-8 says:

> [6] The voice said, "Cry out!"
> And he said, "What shall I cry?"
>
> "All flesh *is* grass,
> and all its loveliness *is* like the flower of the field.
>
> [7] The grass withers, the flower fades,
> because the breath of the LORD blows upon it.
> Surely the people *are* grass.
>
> [8] The grass withers, the flower fades,
> but the Word of our God stands forever." (NKJV)

John 17:3 says: "And this is eternal life, that they may know You, the only true God and Jesus Christ Whom You have sent."

Philippians 3:10 says: "That I may know Him and the power of His resurrection, and the fellowship of His sufferings, being conformed to His death."

For thousands of years, God has strived to reveal Himself to His created beings made in His image. Consider the incredible lengths He has gone to make it impossible for us to deny His existence and presence. Consider also that we were created to reflect Him, His image to each other. Sadly, instead of reflecting the pure and perfect image of God, we have chosen to reflect the image of His enemy who has stolen this world — a world that was created and meant to be our Father's precious gift to us. We have been such small-thinking, foolish human souls, consumed in our present moments of time and space. Romans 1:18-23 tells us:

> [18] What is revealed is God's anger from Heaven against all the Godlessness and wickedness of people who in their wickedness keep suppressing the truth; [19] because what is known about

God is plain to them since God has made it plain to them. [20] For ever since the creation of the universe His invisible qualities — both His eternal power and His divine nature — have been seen, because they can be understood from what he has made. Therefore, they have no excuse [21] Because, although they know who God is, they do not glorify him as God or thank him. On the contrary, they have become futile in their thinking, and their undiscerning hearts have become darkened. [22] Claiming to be wise, they have become fools! [23] In fact, they have exchanged the glory of the immortal God for mere images, like mortal human beings, birds, animals, or reptiles! (CJB)

Hebrews 1:1-3 says:

[1] God, Who at various times and in various ways spoke in time past to the fathers by the prophets, [2] has in these last days spoken to us by *His* Son, Whom He has appointed heir of all things, through Whom also He made the worlds; [3] Who being the brightness of *His* glory and the express image of His Person, and upholding all things by the Word of His power, when He had by Himself purged our sins, sat down at the right hand of the Majesty on high." (NKJV)

This evidence provided by God is irrefutable when we take just a few of these examples: the Bible, our bodies, the whole of creation around us, our conscience, our consciousness, life itself, and the indescribable giving of His Son!

Just take one of these for now; the Bible is the only Book on our Earth that describes how this world came into being and how it will all end. But then it goes so much further by describing how an entirely new creation, a new Heaven, and a new Earth will be brought into being by, through, and for Christ. Consider the hundreds of Bible prophecies that have already been fulfilled and are now in this present time. Consider also that we are witnessing on a global scale the fulfillment of more biblical prophecies than in any other time in the brief history of humanity. Never before have we had to come face to face with such a real possibility of self-annihilation. God is warning us daily through these prophecies coming to pass before our eyes.

An Explosion of Evil

I will ask one question: "How do we explain the explosion of evil that has now gripped our world?" One only has to read Revelation 12 to get the answer.

> [1] Now a great sign appeared in Heaven: a woman clothed with the sun, with the moon under her feet, and on her head a garland of twelve stars. [2] Then being with child, she cried out in labor and in pain to give birth.
>
> [3] And another sign appeared in Heaven: behold, a great, fiery red dragon having seven heads and ten horns, and seven diadems on his heads. [4] His tail drew a third of the stars of Heaven and threw them to the Earth. And the dragon stood before the woman who was ready to give birth, to devour her Child as soon as it was born. [5] She bore a male Child Who was to rule all nations with a rod of iron. And her Child was caught up to God and His throne. [6] Then the woman fled into the wilderness, where she has a place prepared by God, that they should feed her there one thousand two hundred and sixty days.
>
> [7] **And war broke out in Heaven: Michael and his angels fought with the dragon; and the dragon and his angels fought,** [8] **but they did not prevail, nor was a place found for them in Heaven any longer.** [9] **So, the great dragon was cast out, that serpent of old, called the Devil and Satan, who**

deceives the whole world; he was cast to the Earth, and his angels were cast out with him.

[10] **Then I heard a loud voice saying in Heaven, "Now salvation, and strength, and the Kingdom of our God, and the power of His Christ have come, for the accuser of our brethren, who accused them before our God day and night, has been cast down.** [11] And they overcame him by the blood of the Lamb and by the word of their testimony, and they did not love their lives to the death. [12] Therefore rejoice, O heavens, and you who dwell in them! Woe to the inhabitants of the Earth and the sea! For the devil has come down to you, having great wrath, because he knows that he has a short time."

[13] Now when the dragon saw that he had been cast to the Earth, he persecuted the woman who gave birth to the male *Child*. [14] But the woman was given two wings of a great eagle, that she might fly into the wilderness to her place, where she is nourished for a time and times and half a time, from the presence of the serpent. [15] So the serpent spewed water out of his mouth like a flood after the woman, that he might cause her to be carried away by the flood. [16] But the Earth helped the woman, and the Earth opened its mouth and swallowed up the flood which the dragon had spewed out of his mouth. [17] And the dragon was enraged with the woman, and he went to make war with the rest of her offspring, who keep the commandments of God and have the testimony of Jesus Christ. (NKJV)

All the answers to what is happening in our current world are there in our Bibles open for all to see. Finally, we can understand what Jesus was talking about when He said in Matthew 24 that unless He comes back, "No flesh will be saved." Christ must return to save us from ourselves, or we are hopeless.

We humans have perfected one art and that is the art of self-destruction. We have become masters at it. We have reached a state in which man considers himself at the height of maturity, or as some would say, "We have evolved." **In truth, the opposite has taken place**; the more we learn, the more we *devolve*. That is why, for the first time in human history, we are on the brink of wiping ourselves out.

Look at the political worldwide landscape. Here are at least four ways we could annihilate ourselves:

1. The Great Reset. The Illuminati—one new world order telling us, as a matter of fact, that the planet can only survive with 500 million people on it, and of course, it is them that should be the exclusive chosen ones. Therefore, we must rid ourselves of you "useless, polluting, less educated, dirty herd," and all by 2030.

2. China. It is foretold in Revelation 9 and Revelation 16 in one of the most descriptive Bible prophecies written that describe not only China killing one-third of humankind but exactly how they will do it. These prophecies tell us of an army of 200 million. Their colors will be in these dimensions: red, blue, and sulfur (yellow). Check for yourself the colors of the Chinese Air Force and Navy. The Prophecy calls them the kings of the east and tells of them crossing the river Euphrates (look this up as well).

3. Islam has brazenly declared to the world that they won't rest until they eradicate Israel, then America, then the Christians, then the rest of the world in *Jihad*.

4. A.I. — Now we have the greatest threat to civilization, as declared to us by the Earth's richest man, Elon Musk, who is also leading this field of A.I.

At the same time, what is wrong with us? What has gone so horribly wrong with our world for us to be on this precipice of self-destruction?

The answer is quite simple: we have pushed away and denied:

The Source of Life, the Source of Peace, the Source of Love,

YESHUA MESSIAH - Jesus the Christ - The Savior of our fallen world.

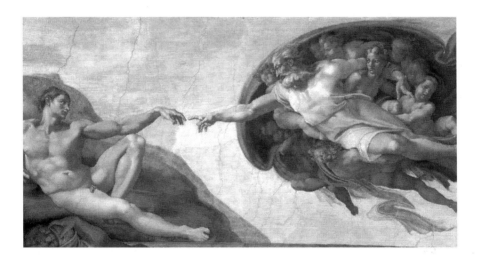

Sistine Chapel

The great artist Michelangelo captured it all perfectly when he painted the ceiling of the Sistine Chapel with this centerpiece. Go and look at the grand picture of God's outstretched arm wanting to touch man with His presence and reality, and then see the man lying there with His hand limp-wrist that asks, "Can I be bothered?" Michelangelo has aptly shown our general attitude toward the Creator Who made us and to Whom we owe everything, not only this life but also eternal life with Him.

The most astonishing, breathtaking, and barely believable part of all this: *El Shaddai,* God Almighty, wants to spend eternity with each one of us, even me. If that is not the most undervalued, misunderstood, underappreciated fact in the entire universe, I don't know what is.

Because we are confined to our human bodies and space and time, in which we only have five senses, and confined to this world, we have great difficulty in understanding the:

INFINITE (boundless)
OMNIPRESENT (everywhere all the time)
OMNIPOTENT (all-powerful)
OMNISCIENT (all-knowing)
SELFLESS LOVE (not unconditional)
ABSOLUTE (self-sufficient One, self-existent One)
PURE (unpolluted, undefiled, uncorrupted, unadulterated)
PERFECT
HOLY
RIGHTEOUS
NOBLE (never does or says anything that is not perfect in its application)
COMPLETE (nothing missing)
THE SOURCE OF ALL LIFE
SELF-EXISTING-SELF-RELIANT
ELOHIM-CREATOR, SOVEREIGN, TRIUNE
JEHOVAH- LORD
EL SHADDAI- GOD ALMIGHTY
ADONAI- LORD, MASTER
JEHOVAH- JIREH-PREVISION and PROVISION
JEHOVAH- ROPHE-HE WHO HEALS
ADONAI- TZVA'OT- LORD OF HOSTS/ARMIES
JEHOVAH- NISSI MY BANNER
JEHOVAH- M'KADDESH HE WHO SANCTIFIES

JEHOVAH- SHALOM PEACE
JEHOVAH- TSIDKENU OUR RIGHTEOUSNESS
JEHOVAH- ROHI MY SHEPHERD
JEHOVAH- SHAMMAH GOD IS THERE

How do we start to bring everything into the proper perspective? We are so imprisoned in our bodies, minds, and seen world. How do we register the difference between the Being, Whose attributes are listed above, and us with all our human frailties and inadequacies and our total smallness?

Even if a man or a woman gained our entire world and all its riches and possessions, it would be a small achievement compared to eternity with our infinite omnipotent God. He would earn a piece of dandruff.

We should ask ourselves this one question: What is the highest achievement a human can reach in one's lifetime? Is it fame, fortune, acceptance, the Nobel Peace Prize, or the presidency of a great country? No. It is none of these. The highest achievement is available to all.

It all comes down to one thing: *our relationship with our CREATOR.* **The only thing that will matter in eternity is our relationship to our Creator.**

Think about the inconsequential things we make so prominent in our lives. Think of them in terms of eternity, then think how small they are. Think about what encompasses our thoughts and consumes us daily, the minuscule dandruff we spend obsessing with our time and thoughts. Do they have any real value? They are worthless if they are not eternal because they will all pass away.

Stop and Weigh

Stop and weigh this: God wants to share all He is and all He has with us, mere insects. Everything that we see and know here on our planet pales in significance compared to being with Him for eternity.

Why, oh why, would we ever do anything that would jeopardize our inheritance? Why would we do anything that would put this unfathomable relationship at risk? To forsake God for the world's temporary pleasures is our willful separation from Him. *Separation from God for eternity* should make one want to shudder at any thoughts of the horrors and damnation facing each one of us.

There is No Such Thing as Eternal Security

Many Christians rest on the doctrine of eternal security, and many variations are wrong. My friend was raised in the Bible Belt of the southern United States. In that place, eternal security was the idea that if somewhere your mother got you to repeat a prayer inviting Jesus into your heart when you were four years old, it made no difference what you did after that because, *once saved, always saved.* You could murder your parents and meditate on the Bible as you renounced God. But you "prayed the prayer," so, *once saved, always saved.* Too bad for you; if you want to go to Hell, you can't.

For others, it's not quite that bad. Others believe that if you walk away from Christ after once committing to following Him, *then you never really were saved, no matter what it looked like.* I'm sympathetic to this version of the doctrine, but it still complicates the matter. The fact is you could have followed Him your whole life. If only you had died when you were following Him, you'd have been with Him for eternity. But for some reason, you made yourself a god and walked away. You have lost what you had.

As I have previously mentioned, in the New Testament, I have found 104 direct references that state that Christians can lose their salvation. "Once saved, always saved" is a myth, a lie from the father of lies. I can give this list to anyone that may want it. One of the clearest is Hebrews 10:26-31:

> [26] For if we sin willfully after we have received the knowledge of the truth, there no longer remains a sacrifice for sins, [27] but a certain fearful expectation of judgment, and fiery indignation which will devour the adversaries. [28] Anyone who has rejected Moses' law dies without mercy on *the testimony of* two or three witnesses. [29] Of how much worse punishment, do you suppose, will he be thought worthy who has trampled the Son of God underfoot, counted the blood of the covenant by which he was sanctified a common thing, and insulted the Spirit of grace? [30] For we know Him Who said, "Vengeance is Mine, I will repay," says the Lord. And again, "The LORD will judge His people." [31] It is a fearful thing to fall into the hands of the living God.

Man's Five Senses

Humans have five senses provided by God. We are hardwired with these to come to an understanding and, ultimately, a deep relationship with Him. We are given these tools of perception so we can *know* Him.

[37] Jesus said to him, "You shall love the Lord your God with all your heart, with all your soul, and with all your mind." (Mt 22:37 NKJV). The Creator has given us these senses so that we should go after the knowledge of Him with all our might, mind, soul, and strength and so that we should come to know and love Him just for Who He is and *not what we can get from Him.*

We should ache to see God in everything we encounter by seeing Him in everything that surrounds us, pining to hear His voice clearly, longing for His tender touch, smelling the sweet aroma of His Being that brings life to life, and tasting every good gift He offers us.

In every situation we encounter, Christians should look for God's presence rather than just bumbling headlong in without stopping to think. We should ask:

Does this look right? Can I see God in this?

Do the Words of Jesus apply here?

Does it feel right? Is the presence of God here?

Does this smell right? Does it have the aroma of God or the stench of the enemy?

Can you taste, and does it taste good? Is there good fruit to be had here?

We have all been given five senses: sight, smell, hearing, taste, and touch.

Consider that God gave us only these five senses. Now consider that there are animals with even more senses than we have and some with much more acute senses than we have. Even a dolphin has one more sense than us; they have sonar, as do bats and whales. How many senses do we think God may have? Could it possibly be in the millions? And how acute would His senses be? If God has so many more senses than man, and we consider the sight of an eagle or the smelling power of a dog or shark, how acute must the senses be of the Creator that gave each animal its senses?

At any moment, 8 billion people on the planet have thoughts. At any given millisecond, there is no single human thought that the Creator is not intimately aware of. Scripture tells us that even every sparrow that falls to the ground, God is mindful of (Mt 10:29), and every hair on the head of every person who lives and has ever lived, He knows. (Lk 12:7)

How Then Should We Fellowship

When we come together in fellowship, let it be for us to use all our senses as Jesus did. Let's look through His filter and see Christ in each other. Let's hear the Voice of God in all our conversations and discern His Words. Let's smell the aroma of life to life. Let's go past touching the hem of His garment, touch Him physically, let His virtue flow into us, and fill our bodies with healing and joy through His Holy Spirit. Let's taste Jesus by eating His body, "the Word made flesh," and drink His blood, "the blood of forgiveness, grace, and mercy."

CHAPTER 2:

PRAYER: INTIMACY WITH GOD

How Do We Finite Beings Communicate with an Infinite Spirit?

Blessed are those servants whom the Master, when he comes, will find watching. Assuredly, I say to you that He will gird Himself and have them sit down to eat and will come and serve them. (Lk 12:37)

I once attended a wedding in Israel. There, they have a special occasion one week after the marriage to celebrate with the son in his marriage to his new bride.

I observed an interaction after this Jewish celebration that hit me right in the heart. We were all standing around talking, and Thomas, the groom, the son of Moshe (Moses), reached out and cupped his father's cheek with his hand. Then Thomas took his hand and kissed his fingers before sending that kiss to God. I had never witnessed anything even remotely like this before. I was amazed and more than touched by what I saw. God has blessed the Jewish people to understand relationships and affection in a way we Westerners rarely, if ever, see.

For me, it was a wake-up call to experience how deep relationships can be, and are, embedded in the DNA of the Hebrew people. This DNA is God-given. After the ceremony, we left the synagogue, and as we walked down the street, I was walking behind Moshe and Thomas, and I watched them walk down the road together, hand in hand. It was pure affection between a father and a son.

I immediately thought of the story of the woman caught in adultery dragged before Jesus. As I contemplated that scene, the Lord gave me a picture of how the interaction played out between Jesus, the accusers, and the woman caught in the act of adultery.

When all the accusation and embarrassment had finished, and the accusers had left, Jesus would have cupped the face of the adulteress with His calloused hands and gently lifted her to her feet. He would have stared into her eyes and said, *"Go and sin no more."* Picture this in your mind. He is our gentle and affectionate God.

Can you imagine that woman ever committing that same sin again? Jesus is calling us to this place where He can cup *our* faces in His hands and say with tender sincerity, *"Go and sin no more." This* is relationship.

Have you ever had the amazing experience of cupping a baby's face, and immediately that baby pulls her shoulder up and closes your hand onto her shoulder because of the comfort and security you have brought her? That is how it is meant to be between us and our Father.

This connection reminds me of the American people (I myself am an Aussie). Americans are the most respectful and courteous people I have ever encountered, which I believe comes from their Judeo-Christian roots. Also, many Americans I have met, like the Jewish people, greatly understand genuine affection. I pray they do not lose that.

AFFECTIONATE PRAYER

I was *blessed* many years ago, around 1995, to have gone through three years of depression.

It is challenging to comprehend depression as a blessing because we humans immediately jump to the conclusion that depression can only be a bad thing. "What depression is a blessing?" This is because we continually focus on the life of the "here and now." But the "here and now" is a blip in eternity.

These three years completely changed my life. It changed my walk and relationship with my Savior, which changed how I communicated with Him. As Jesus ever so gently led me through the black hole of despair, He taught me daily to only trust and rely on Him. At the time, He gave me this Scripture from Isaiah, "Put on the garments of Praise for the Spirit of heaviness." (Isa 61:3)

I made this Scripture the essence of my life in Him.

I would not be the man I am today or have the relationship with Him I have today were it not for those three years of blessing. When I say that prayer is a relationship with Him, I came by this understanding through my suffering. He was my lifeline, my everything, and while it was brutal at the time, the sweetness of what came out of it made it a thousand times worth the pain.

THE NAMES OF JESUS

As mentioned in the previous chapter, Jesus has 250-300 names and titles in Scripture. During my depression, He would lead me daily through some of these unique names and titles, showing me exactly how each one of them applied to me in my life and exactly what each one of these titles meant to me personally. Then, each day, Jesus would faithfully take me by the collar, lift me out of the pit, and place me upright on the ground.

As I applied each title and what it meant to me, I could feel the wrinkled frown grow into a smile that went from ear to ear on my face until, at the end of the three years, He healed me completely. The result was that Jesus had built a completely different person.

I know why He allowed me to go through this for three years; it was because of my nature and my self-reliance that He needed to allow this amount of time so that I could escape this prison of selfishness. Then, Christ gave me the vast bonus of teaching me to fall more deeply in love with Him each day, becoming more intimate in knowing Him.

The Titles of God the Son

Were you aware that Jesus has 250 to 300 titles and names that are applied to Him throughout Scripture and that He is like no other sovereign in history? We have heard the names of other kings, such as "Richard the Lionheart," "Alexander the Great," and "Ivan the Terrible." These titles they have given to themselves or were given by their subjects. But all the titles of Christ were given to Him by His Father. Take the following, just a few of His titles and names, and apply them to your life and your person. Consider what each of these titles means to you personally in your relationship with Him.

Please ask for God's presence and take your time.

SUFFERING SERVANT
GREAT REDEEMER
AUTHOR and FINISHER OF LIFE
AUTHOR AND FINISHER OF FAITH.
GREAT HIGH PRIEST

CHIEF APOSTLE
GOD THE SON
ONLY BEGOTTEN GOD
SON OF GOD
THE CHRIST
THE CAPTAIN OF THE LORD'S ARMY
MELCHIZIDEK - KING OF RIGHTEOUSNESS
MESSIAH
SAVIOR
LIGHT OF THE WORLD
THE LIFE OF MEN
WORD OF GOD
WORD MADE FLESH
THE HOLY ONE OF ISRAEL
THE ANOINTED ONE
THE LAMB OF GOD
CREATOR
BELOVED SON
KING OF KINGS
LORD OF LORDS
HEAD OF THE CHURCH
THE ALMIGHTY
HIGH PRIEST
THE FIRST AND LAST (ALPHA AND OMEGA)
THE TRUE SHEPHERD
THE GOOD SHEPHERD

Now take just one of these blessed names, the Suffering Servant, and meditate on it. The relationship the Suffering Servant desires with us is one where we just adore Jesus, His purity, nobility, righteousness, and holiness. If you look back into His tender eyes as He cups your face, you will find there is nothing else. A prayer life is a relationship. A prayer is an intimate two-way conversation with the lover of our soul.

When we meditate on the Suffering Servant, we will experience Him intimately. We must look to Scripture to adequately capture the essence of this name.

John 13 to 17:

I won't print these here, but please love yourself enough to open the Word of God next to this book and feast on these chapters. These Scriptures are the "last will and testament" of our Lord Jesus, THE SUFFERING SERVANT, given the night before He was crucified. When we read through these, we see how selfless our God is. Throughout these passages, His *only* concern was for His disciples–His friends, and for us, His future saints and bride-to-be. These are my favorite Scriptures in the Bible because they display the inside and heart of MESSIAH YESHUA.

Psalm 22:

This is the great prophetic Psalm about the crucifixion and the suffering that our Lord endured on the cross, and it bears printing here.

> [1] My God, My God, why have You forsaken Me?
> *Why are You so* far from helping Me,
> *and from* the words of My groaning?
>
> [2] O My God, I cry in the daytime, but You do not hear;
> and in the night season and am not silent.
>
> [3] But You *are* holy,
> enthroned in the praises of Israel.
>
> [4] Our fathers trusted in You;
> they trusted, and You delivered them.
>
> [5] They cried to You, and were delivered;
> they trusted in You, and were not ashamed.

[6] But I *am* a worm, and no man;
a reproach of men, and despised by the people.

[7] All those who see Me ridicule Me;
they shoot out the lip, they shake the head, *saying,*

[8] "He trusted in the LORD, let Him rescue Him;
let Him deliver Him, since He delights in Him!"

[9] But You *are* He Who took Me out of the womb;
You made Me trust *while* on My mother's breasts.

[10] I was cast upon You from birth.
From My mother's womb,
You *have been* My God.

[11] Be not far from Me,
for trouble *is* near;
for *there is* none to help.

[12] Many bulls have surrounded Me;
strong *bulls* of Bashan have encircled Me.

[13] They gape at Me *with* their mouths,
like a raging and roaring lion.

[14] I am poured out like water,
and all My bones are out of joint.
My heart is like wax;

it has melted within Me.

[16] My strength is dried up like a potsherd,
and My tongue clings to My jaws.
You have brought Me to the dust of death.

[16] For dogs have surrounded Me;
the congregation of the wicked has enclosed Me.
They pierced My hands and My feet.

[17] I can count all My bones.
They look *and* stare at Me.

[18] They divide My garments among them,
and for My clothing they cast lots.

[19] But You, O LORD, do not be far from Me;
O My Strength, hasten to help Me!

[20] Deliver Me from the sword,
my precious *life* from the power of the dog.

[21] Save Me from the lion's mouth
and from the horns of the wild oxen!

You have answered Me.

[22] I will declare Your name to My brethren.
In the midst the assembly I will praise You.

[23] You who fear the LORD, praise Him!
All you descendants of Jacob, glorify Him,
and fear Him, all you offspring of Israel!

[24] For He has not despised nor abhorred the affliction of the
afflicted; nor has He hidden His face from Him.
But when He cried to Him, He heard.

[25] My praise *shall be* of You in the great assembly;
I will pay My vows before those who fear Him.

[26] The poor shall eat and be satisfied;
those who seek Him will praise the LORD.
Let your heart live forever!

[27] All the ends of the world
shall remember and turn to the LORD,
and all the families of the nations
shall worship before You.

[28] For the kingdom *is* the LORD's,
and He rules over the nations.

[29] All the prosperous of the Earth
shall eat and worship.
All those who go down to the dust
shall bow before Him,
even he who cannot keep himself alive.

[30] A posterity shall serve Him.
It will be recounted of the Lord to the *next* generation.

[31] They will come and declare His righteousness to a people
who will be born, that He has done *this*.

This, again, is from the inside of Jesus. The Psalmist speaks about what
He would be going through, what He would be thinking, the anguish,
grief, and pain as He took on Himself the sins of the world, the wrath
of His Father, the shame of the cross, defeating and crushing the
enemy.

**Picture This: Five category five tornadoes are bearing down on
Jesus all at once as He hung on the cross. He had taken on
Himself:**

1) the sins of the world,
2) separation from His Father for the first time in all eternity,
3) the wrath of His Father,
4) the shame of the cross,
5) and the defeating and crushing of the enemy.

Consider that this Psalm of David was written approximately 1,000
years before the time of Jesus and yet contains pinpoint accuracy about
the events that took place 1,000 years after David wrote it. Crucifixion
had not yet been invented. It was to become the worst form of a

degrading, humiliating, painful execution invented and introduced by Satan through the Romans.

Go and read Isaiah 52:13, and Isaiah 53. These verses from Isaiah present a vivid description of the suffering Jesus went through to pay for our sins. Isaiah prophesied approximately 700 years before our Lord's time; yet again, we find pinpoint accuracy in every detail. There were 65 individual prophecies to be fulfilled regarding the week of the crucifixion and resurrection of our Lord, and all *were* fulfilled. Many of them concerned His brutal suffering, lovingly endured for the sake of His people.

Isaiah 53:14 says: "Just as many were astonished at you, So His visage was marred more than any man, And His form more than the sons of men."

Jesus was beaten and striped at least five times before He was nailed to the cross. He was almost unrecognizable as a man because of the beatings that were so inhumanely inflicted on Him.

Isaiah 53:3-5 tells us:

> [3] He is despised and rejected by men, A Man of sorrows and acquainted with grief. And we hid, as it were, *our* faces from Him; He was despised, and we did not esteem Him. [4] Surely, He has borne our griefs and carried our sorrows; Yet we esteemed Him stricken, Smitten by God, and afflicted. [5] But He *was* wounded for our transgressions, *He was* bruised for our iniquities; the chastisement for our peace *was* upon Him, And by His stripes, we are healed.

TYPICAL PRAYER LIFE

"God, here is my list of prayer needs. Could you please attend to these?"

Let's consider the typical prayer life. More importantly, let's consider your own. Does it go something like the above? Is God a genie in a bottle? From our youth, many of us learned to pray using constructed, repetitive prayer, continually asking for the same thing in parrot fashion, or even just saying one word repeatedly, such as "Hallelujah," as though it were some incantation.

Picture this: You are excited to go and spend quality time with your adult son you have not seen in months. He told you he has something important to talk to you about. You feel glad that he still comes to you with important things. He sits across from you at the diner you always took him to since he was a boy. You've ordered pancakes for both of you and are sipping hot coffee while waiting for the waitress to bring them. He says, "Dad, I need your help."

You open your mouth to respond. You are about to say, "Sure, son, what do you need?" But before you can say anything, he says, "Dad, I need your help."

Again, you are about to respond, and he says, "Dad, I need your help. Dad, I need your help."

"Dad, I need your help.

"Dad, I need your help."

"Dad, Dad, Dad, Father-Dad, Dad, Dad, Dad…"

This continues for some time and it's confusing to you. He finally stops and says, "If it's your will." Then, astonishingly, he leaves the table. The pancakes haven't even arrived, and he walks out of the diner. You are wondering what in the world just happened.

Imagine if someone just called your name or said one word to you over and over and over. How would you feel? You would want them to stop and start engaging in a fulfilling conversation. Most people talk to God this way, just prattling on and not allowing Him to respond to us. This is no way to have a relationship.

All communication should be interactive and mutual and requires a response.

We all have acquaintances who just continually keep talking at us, never allowing for a response. Even worse is when they ask a question, and as you begin to reply, they just jump back in with what they want to say.

This person is hopelessly self-centered (I exaggerate. Many of us have been able to overcome this somewhat by the grace of God). They consider themselves far more important than you and likely seek relationships for the sake of stroking their own egos. How will you respond to all they are telling you? That's what their hearts want to know. What do you think of all they are saying? It is an inward-focused heart. Is this how we want to approach God?

Even when we come together for corporate prayer, we all bring our lists, needs, wants, and petitions to God. Shouldn't we be polite and see what the Holy God would like to say first by reading His Word, the Words of Jesus?

If you knew someone and every time you spoke to them, they just asked you for something or expected something from you, you would feel you were being used. It would become so tedious it would wear you out physically and mentally, and you would begin looking for ways to avoid them.

Those who interact selfishly with God can even become rude, making declarations and placing themselves above God while making commands. I have heard many people praying, making declarations such as "I bind" and "I declare," and then sometimes, to cover their paths, they will add Jesus into the picture: "I declare, in Jesus' name!" Remember, *without Him, "we can do nothing."* He is the One to make declarations.

Conversation Between the Finite and the Infinite

How do I, a finite being, contact and communicate with an infinite Spirit? First, I must understand that I cannot—apart from His grace and help. John 15:5 says: "For without Me you can do nothing."

We must go to Him. We must adopt the disciplined prayer life that has been laid out in the simple, pure guidelines given to us by Jesus. Only in this way will we achieve the following in our relationship with the triune God, Son, and Holy Spirit.

We will understand the majesty and sovereignty of Jesus Christ.

We will understand our position in Him.

We will understand our relationship with our Heavenly Father.

We will understand entering His rest.

We will understand being part of a Royal Priesthood.

We will understand our Great High Priest.

We will understand reaching the Holiest of Holies and then praying out from that place.

We will understand how God gets His rest in us because of our obedience.

We will understand Jesus in comparison to even the greatest of human beings, who all pale into insignificance compared to Him.

We will learn to hear clearly from Him.

In short, so much of what we can understand about our Creator depends on our willingness to understand and engage in our relationship with Him through the gift of prayer. Matthew 11:27-30 says:

> [27] All things have been delivered to Me by My Father, and no one knows the Son except the Father. Nor does anyone know the Father except the Son, and *the one* to whom the Son wills to reveal *Him.*[28] Come to Me, all *you* who labor and are heavy laden, and I will give you rest. [29] Take My yoke upon you and learn from Me, for I am gentle and lowly in heart, and you will find rest for your souls. [30] For My yoke *is* easy, and My burden is light." (NKJV)

Matthew 6:6 says:

> But you, when you pray, go into your room, and when you have shut your door, pray to your Father Who is in the secret place; and your Father Who sees in secret will reward you openly.

It is vital to our walk and relationship with God that we apply His rules to our lives, and particularly, our prayer life, which includes the following:

- Understanding how God requires us to approach Him in prayer.
- Knowing where Jesus wants to take us in prayer.
- Realizing Who we are praying to and how we approach each of the Three Persons of the Godhead (in the next chapter).

In this way, we will see Him answer prayer, but infinitely more importantly, we will live out the relationship we were created for and will enjoy to greater and greater degrees in this life and especially in the life to come. In the following two chapters, we will explore the topic of prayer and intimacy with God more thoroughly.

CHAPTER 3:
COMMUNION WITH GOD IN THE HOLY OF HOLIES

How Do We Have Union with Him?

In the last chapter, we began to explore prayer as a union with God in Christ. We looked at the intimacy Jesus desires with us as we learn to come to God for a mutual conversation and relationship.

In this chapter, we will explore:

1. Praying into and out from the Holiest of Holies

2. Communion – Common Union – to unite with God through your prayer life

3. Prayer without ceasing

4. Human relationships

Like Jesus in the Holiest Place

God made us in His image; therefore, in the same manner as Jesus did, we should approach Holy God.

Go through the Scriptures to see how the priesthood were required to prepare themselves and the temple before they dared approach the Great I Am. There was step upon step of ritual cleansing, a religious exercise that intensely trained the Jewish consciousness in the relationship between sinful man and Holy God. Did the rituals make them holy? No. God made them holy. But the rituals taught them.

Many will say, "But we now live under the new covenant, and it is all different now!" Is it? This begs the question: Has God changed? Read Jeremiah 31 and Hebrews 8 and 10 to truly identify with this new blood covenant and the price that has now been paid so that we can enter this new covenant and relationship. Here is some of it:

> [31] "Behold, the days are coming," says the LORD, "when I will make a new covenant with the house of Israel and with the house of Judah— [32] not according to the covenant that I made with their fathers in the day *that* I took them by the hand to lead them out of the land of Egypt, My covenant which they broke, though I was a husband to them," says the LORD. [33] "But this *is* the covenant that I will make with the house of Israel after those days," says the LORD. "I will put My law in their minds, and write it on their hearts; and I will be their God, and they shall be My people. [34] No more shall every man teach his neighbor, and every man his brother, saying, 'Know the LORD,' for they all shall know Me, from the least of them to the greatest of them," says the LORD. "For I will forgive their iniquity, and their sin I will remember no more." (Jer 31:31-34 NKJV)

And in the New Testament:

[1] Now *this is* the main point of the things we are saying: We have such a high priest, who is seated at the right hand of the throne of the Majesty in the heavens, [2] a minister of the sanctuary and of the true tabernacle which the Lord erected, and not man.

[3] For every high priest is appointed to offer both gifts and sacrifices. Therefore, *it is* necessary that this one also has something to offer. [4] For if he were on Earth, he would not be a priest, since there are priests who offer the gifts according to the law; [5] who serve the copy and shadow of the heavenly things, as Moses was divinely instructed when he was about to make the tabernacle. For he said, "See *that* you make all things according to the pattern shown you on the mountain." [6] But now he has obtained a more excellent ministry, since he is also mediator of a better covenant, which was established on better promises.

[7] For if that first *covenant* had been faultless, then no place would have been sought for a second. [8] Because finding fault with them, He says: "Behold, the days are coming," says the LORD, "when I will make a new covenant with the house of Israel and with the house of Judah— [9] not according to the covenant that I made with their fathers in the day when I took them by the hand to lead them out of the land of Egypt; because they did not continue in My covenant, and I disregarded them," says the LORD. [10] "For this *is* the covenant that I will make with the house of Israel after those days, says the LORD: "I will put My laws in their mind and write them on their hearts; and I will be their God, and they shall be My people. [11] None of them shall teach his neighbor, and none his brother, saying, 'Know the

LORD,' for all shall know Me, from the least of them to the greatest of them. [12] For I will be merciful to their unrighteousness, and their sins and their lawless deeds I will remember no more."

[13] In that He says, "A new *covenant*," He has made the first obsolete. Now what is becoming obsolete and growing old is ready to vanish away. (Heb 8:1-13 NKJV)

And in Hebrews 10:11-18 (NKJV):

[11] And every priest stands ministering daily and offering repeatedly the same sacrifices, which can never take away sins. [12] But this Man, after He had offered one sacrifice for sins forever, sat down at the right hand of God, [13] from that time waiting till His enemies are made His footstool. [14] For by one offering He has perfected forever those who are being sanctified.

[15] But the Holy Spirit also witnesses to us; for after He had said before,

[16] "This *is* the covenant that I will make with them after those days," says the LORD. "I will put My laws into their hearts, and in their minds I will write them." [17] Then *He adds,* "Their sins and their lawless deeds I will remember no more." [18] Now, where there is remission of these, *there is* no longer an offering for sin.

Do you see the parallels between the way God, Who never changes, is presented in both the Old and New Testaments? We are now a Royal Priesthood and Vessels in which God I Holy Spirit resides. This can be seen clearly in the book of Hosea.

Hosea wrote to the Jews, but this promise applies to us as well. We are the betrothed of Jesus Christ and grafted into His blood covenant. The thing I love about the book of Hosea is we see the King of all Creation laying His heart bare for all to see and understand. Hosea 2:16 says: *"And it shall be, in that day,"* says the Lord, *"that you will call Me 'My Husband,' and no longer call Me 'My Master.'"*

Today in our societies, God has been portrayed dreadfully, and the portrayal is getting worse daily. The enemy is lying. Stop yourself and ponder just one thought: *You will be married to the Infinite One for eternity.* Let's undertake to understand God in His Majesty so we will understand how to approach Him as His bride, which He requires us to do.

Isaiah 66:1-2 says:

> [1] Thus says the LORD:

> > "Heaven *is* My throne,
> > and Earth *is* My footstool.
> > Where *is* the house that you will build Me?
> > And where *is* the place of My rest?

> > [2] For all those *things* My hand has made,
> > and all those *things* exist,"
> > Says the LORD.
> > "But on this *one* will I look
> > on *him who is* poor and of a contrite spirit,
> > and who trembles at My Word." (NKJV)

His rest in us should be our daily goal, first and foremost, simply because He is God. Then, through the correct approach to Him, we can reach our rest in Him. This rest is at the heart of our eternal, loving relationship with Him.

[15] For thus says the Lord GOD, the Holy One of Israel:

> "In returning and rest you shall be saved;
> in quietness and confidence shall be your strength.
> But you would not." (Isa 30:15)

He is our rest because of our obedience, love, and adoration toward Him. But we can become His rest. God is at ease with us, which is the opposite of the manufactured disease (Dis-Ease) He has with the world He created to be His rest. True prayer occurs when we rest in God, *and* He rests in us.

HOLY OF HOLIES

When God stretched out His mighty hand to rescue His children from slavery in Egypt, He brought them into the wilderness to refine them for forty years before giving them their Promised Land. It was in the wilderness that He instructed Moses to build a tabernacle for worship, a copy of a Heavenly Throne Room. The original tabernacle and the subsequent three latter temples, Solomon's temple, Nehemiah/Ezra's temple, and Herod's temple, all had three separate parts:

1. The Outer Court/Court of the Gentiles
2. The Inner Court/the Holy Place
3. Holy of Holy Place within the Holy Place

This is a *pattern* of the true and better Resting place and Holy of Holies. The Old Testament is full of patterns for what is real and heavenly, and even for Christ Himself. These are also called *types*. The Holy of Holies in the tabernacle and temples is a pattern for God's true dwelling in His people and His Church.

Reaching that place of rest in Jesus Christ through prayer can only come when we are yoked with Him in partnership. We move through the Court of the Gentiles into the Holy Place, then even closer into the Holy of Holies.

The Court of the Gentiles

We read in Scripture that Jesus, twice, in great anger, took a whip and drove the thieves and money changers out of the Court of the Gentiles because the Pharisees, priests, and Sadducees were hindering the Gentiles who wanted to find God from doing so. Many do not realize that God always made provision for the proselyte, the genuine seeker who, though not a Jew, was a lover of the God of the Jews. The Court of the Gentiles was where they could worship Him.

But when Jesus was driven to such anger, He found the Court of the Gentiles all set up like a temple mafia. It was all about getting money out of God-seeking people who had journeyed from many different nations hoping to contact the One True God of the Universe.

The church leaders had a lucrative system going that you had to have a particular temple currency which they controlled. A seeker of God had to have his animals and his grain to offer as a sacrifice. But he couldn't just bring one; it all had to come through the religious establishment and at a considerable profit for the establishment and the vendors. But God never intended any of this. He has always required and insisted upon a One-on-one relationship with each of us. This insistence on standing between seekers and the God they sought was a bastardization of the idea of a priestly mediator.

Because of the complexity of our modern lives that are so full of the world, we will have to do precisely the same thing in our prayer lives as Jesus did in the temple court. We will have to pray past ourselves, our surroundings, and our mundane lives that are so cluttered with cares.

We will have to overturn the tables and drive out what distracts us from coming to our Father, through His Son, and by His Spirit.

It is getting worse daily and will continue to worsen with the increase in technology and humanity being controlled by I.T. and machines. If you are on Facebook, get out. If you are on any media platform, get out. It is all controlled by "the enemy - the prince of the air."

If you must be connected, you must make a choice; either you control it, or it will control you. And if I were to make a judgment, I would have to say from experience that the latter is the case. If so, one simply must disconnect. The media barons will do exactly what the corrupt church leaders did in the days of Christ; they will convince you that you must have their mode of currency to be accepted. This will all but end your prayer life.

Getting Serious

Mark 9:42-50 says:

> [42] "But whoever causes one of these little ones who believe in me to stumble, it would be better for him if a millstone were hung around his neck, and he were thrown into the sea. [43] If your hand causes you to sin, cut it off. It is better for you to enter life maimed, rather than having two hands, to go to Hell, into the fire that shall never be quenched— [44] where:

> 'Their worm does not die,
> and the fire is not quenched.'

> [45] And if your foot causes you to sin, cut it off. It is better for you to enter life lame, rather than having two feet, to be cast into Hell, into the fire that shall never be quenched— [46] where:

> 'Their worm does not die,
> and the fire is not quenched.'

[47] And if your eye causes you to sin, pluck it out. It is better for you to enter the Kingdom of God with one eye, rather than having two eyes, to be cast into Hell fire— [48] where:

> 'Their worm does not die,
> and the fire is not quenched.'

[49] For everyone will be seasoned with fire, and every sacrifice will be seasoned with salt. [50] Salt *is* good, but if the salt loses its flavor, how will you season it? Have salt in yourselves and have peace with one another."

In the time when this passage was written, salt was used for mainly two things: sterilization and fertilization. Jesus commands us to "have salt in" ourselves. For us to have the power within us to sterilize what needs to be stopped and to fertilize what needs to be multiplied, we must "pluck out" whatever "causes [us] to sin." Whatever causes us to lose our saltiness and takes away the keys to the kingdom that have been given to us. (Mt 16:14-19) Without a radical orientation in our lives, we will "lose [our] flavor" and fail to enter the Holy of Holies. For most people, the degree to which they are losing their saltiness is predicated upon the number of hours they spend on these new forms of media. What would be the equivalent of "plucking out an eye?" This is a crucial question.

To Enter In

But removing the distractions (such as "eyes" and "hands") is half the solution. The more critical activity is engagement. We must choose to enter that place. It is not enough to avoid the darkness; we must go into the light.

The High Priest had to undergo meticulous steps to enter the Holy of Holies in the wilderness. In today's dispensation, we must also go through three steps to enter the Holy of Holies in our own regenerated spirit, where the Holy Spirit resides.

Step 1

Make sure that we are always in partnership/yoked with Jesus (Mt 11:28) as set out in the beginning of this chapter. When we get down on our knees, we will be in the *Court of the Gentiles,* and our minds will be so distracted, jumping around from thought to thought and all over the place, beset with such mundane and futile thoughts that don't amount to much (or am I the only one this happens to!).

We will need to gird up the loins of our minds (1 Pt?). We may or will, on many occasions, need to take a whip to these thoughts and drive them out of our minds in the name of Jesus. Depending on how much you practice concentration, this could take some time. Turn your mind to God again and again. The distracting thoughts will come less frequently.

Step 2

We have left the Court of the Gentiles and will now enter the *Holy Place* where we will start to pray for the needs of others and our daily needs. This entering is a good thing to do and should not be undervalued. It is acceptable to God. The problem occurs when we get up from the Holy Place and go out without tasting the Holy of Holies. But Jesus wants us to keep coming to be with Him. He calls us to move past the Court of the Gentiles and then move past the Holy Place.

Step 3

We will reach and pray into and then out from the *Holiest Place* in partnership with Him. Then, and only then, will our prayers have their full divine impact. The only way that we, His betrothed, can drive our prayers through the Court of the Gentiles, through the Holy Place, and into the Holiest Place is to lift Jesus to His rightful place in our minds and hearts by simply dwelling on Him and Him alone.

As I said above, what defeated my three-year depression was meditating in the Holiest Place on His names and titles and what they mean to us individually, meditating on His Person and what He has done for each of us. Dwelling on His complete selflessness, purity, love, righteousness, grace, mercy, and just Who our God is, is the way in.

Dwell on His Words; they are so rich. They are Himself on display.

ACTS

Here is a simple way to remember the steps in our prayer lives. Notice that "self" comes last in this pattern. It's called ACTS, and many have used it to focus their prayer lives for maximum spiritual benefit.

A.C.T.S.

A- Adoration
C- Confession
T- Thanksgiving
S- Supplication

A - We must start all our prayers with adoration, which develops our reverence and relationship with the Father, Son, and Holy Spirit. Remember that Jesus taught us to pray, "Our Father in Heaven...*Hallowed be Your name.*" Adoration, awe, and worship are characteristics of the posture we adopt by faith even as we enter His presence. Sometimes, it will not be by mere faith. If we enter the Holy of Holies, it will be by sight, though not in the sense that it will be by sight when Jesus returns. It will be, rather, awe inspired by our perception of a manifestation of God's holy and awesome presence.

C - Then we can move to confession. We all know that we fall short of the glory of God (Ro 3:10) and have sinfulness in our flesh, but He still loves us intensely. We only need to read Hosea to see this, as mentioned previously. He has made the way by the blood of Jesus for us to confess our sins and be cleansed for our entrance into the Holy Place. Coming into the light of His presence is to come into the light of the truth, not only about Him but about us. Confession of sin is honest and true, and the Lord only accepts those who worship Him in spirit *and in truth*. Confess your sins before Him and receive His loving acceptance and forgiveness. Confession is the only way to receive it.

T - This stands for Thanksgiving. We read in Jeremiah that God says that He not only fills the Earth but also the universe (see Chapter 1: The Omnipresence of God). He is infinite, yet He is in every cell of our body. To say that *we owe Him everything* is the greatest understatement ever uttered. We all have a debt that is impossible to repay, but our Benefactor paid the debt for us. Could there ever be enough words spoken that would truly show our gratitude?

Even the pagans have found by trial and error that a life of gratitude is a "good life." Aside from being God-honoring, there is something deeply transformational in committing to live a life of gratitude. Indeed, no prayer should be without a healthy element of thanksgiving.

S - Last and finally, there is Supplication, in which we pray for the needs of others *and then* our own needs.

James 5:16 says:

> To confess your trespasses to one another, and pray for one another, that you may be healed. The effective, fervent prayer of a righteous man avails much.

The secret to obtaining healing from God is to pray for the healing of others first. The ultimate goal in prayer is for Jesus to take us to be with

Him in the now into that which will become the eternal. Is He not "on the right hand of the Father?" Colossians 3:1 says: "If then you were raised with Christ, seek those things which are above, where Christ is, sitting at the right hand of God."

Ephesians 2:6 says: "…and raised us up together, and made us sit together in the heavenly places in Christ Jesus…"

I must continue quoting the Scriptures because they are the essence of this teaching and are important revelations and instructions from Jesus for each of us.

Matthew 11:27 says:

> All things have been delivered to Me by My Father, and no one knows the Son except the Father. Nor does anyone know the Father except the Son, and the one to whom the Son wills to reveal Him.

We have to partner with Jesus Christ. He, and He alone, can take us to be with Him to the Throne of Grace, the Holy of Holies. Matthew 11:28 says: "Come to Me, all you who labor and are heavy laden, and I will give you rest." Most people think of this as the earthly Christ in the first century calling those in the vicinity to follow Him in His three-year earthly ministry. But I say He is calling out to us from the His throne at the right hand of the Father.

In the same chapter, verses 29 and 30 say:

> Take My yoke (partner with Me) upon you and learn from Me, for I am gentle and lowly in heart, and you will find rest for your souls. For My yoke is easy and My burden is light.

> When you get to this place, the Holiest Place, you will "breathe out" with a sigh of gratitude; you are there: the *rest*.

Carrying the Holy Place into Our Daily Lives

Entering the Holiest Place to be with God is a powerful privilege and experience. But we will learn through this discipline of prayer to get to this Holiest Place while we are in prayer and carry this with us in our daily lives. Then, no matter where we are or in what situation we find ourselves, we can be at rest with and in Him.

Taking His yoke is partnering with Him, not only in prayer but in every aspect of our lives. Then, and only then, when we act and speak, we will ask ourselves, "Is this me or Christ in me?" Just as Jesus claimed He could do nothing apart from His Father, we can do nothing apart from Him and, by extension, His Father and Holy Spirit.

We will never get to the Holiest of Holies in our own strength. We need Jesus to take us there. We will also never do this in our daily living. We need Jesus to do this in our lives as well. All of this will only be made possible through deep intimacy with Him. It has to be about Jesus, not us. He has to take us to this place through the outer court, the Holy Place, and the Holy of Holies. This is Christ's work, but we must invite Him into our hearts to undertake it.

When we reach that place of rest, the Holy of Holies, and pray from there, all our prayers have an impact. They will have the true meaning and power of the great statement in Christ's prayer, "thy will be done on Earth as it is in Heaven." (Lk 11:2)

Our Individual Prayer Life

How often do you consider your individual prayer life? We can stand in the Court of the Gentiles throwing our petitions, wants, and needs at God like throwing rocks through a window; it just doesn't work, and people wonder why they don't hear from God and why He doesn't answer their prayers.

I imagine we also leave God feeling like this: *They didn't even stop to say hello, I love You, or I want to know every deep, intimate part of you.*

We can just come bowling up with our lists and sometimes our commands and demands on JESUS, telling Him how He should run things (this can be downright rude). Hebrews 10:19-23 says:

> [19] Therefore, brethren, having boldness to enter the Holiest by the blood of Jesus, [20] by a new and living way which He consecrated for us, through the veil, that is, His flesh, [21] and having a High Priest over the house of God, [22] let us draw near with a true heart in full assurance of faith, having our hearts sprinkled from an evil conscience and our bodies washed with pure water. Let us hold fast the confession of our hope without wavering, for He Who promised is faithful. (NKJV)

Hebrews 4:1-11 tells us:

> Therefore, since a promise remains of entering His rest, let us fear lest any of you seem to have come short of it. [2] For indeed the gospel was preached to us as well as to them; but the word which they heard did not profit them, not being mixed with faith in those who heard *it.* [3] For we who have believed do enter that rest, as He has said:
>
> > "So I swore in My wrath,
> > 'They shall not enter My rest,'"
>
> although the works were finished from the foundation of the world. [4] For He has spoken in a certain place of the seventh *day* in this way: "And God rested on the seventh day from all His works;" [5] and again in this *place:* "They shall not enter My rest."
>
> [6] Since therefore it remains that some *must* enter it, and those to whom it was first preached did not enter because of

disobedience, [7] Again He designates a certain day, saying in David, "Today," after such a long time, as it has been said:

"Today, if you hear His voice,
do not harden your hearts."

[8] For if Joshua had given them rest, then He would not afterward have spoken of another day. [9] There remains therefore a rest for the people of God. [10] For he who has entered His rest has himself also ceased from his works as God *did* from His. [11] Let us, therefore, be diligent to enter that rest, lest anyone fall according to the same example of disobedience. (NKJV)

The Gospel

**ALL SIN COMES AT A COST.
THERE IS A PRICE THAT HAS TO BE PAID.
YOU CAN EITHER ACCEPT THE PRICE THAT JESUS HAS PAID OR YOU WILL PAY THE PRICE YOURSELF.**

Let's not be confused with "modern theology" that has muddied the waters. There is a judgment coming; there is a Hell; there is a price to be paid for sin. We can have it paid now through the blood of Jesus or pay the price ourselves. Ezekiel 18:4 says: "Behold, all souls are Mine; the soul of the father as well as the soul of the son is Mine; the soul who sins shall die."

When we discipline ourselves to pray in this manner, we will receive true riches and comprehend the context that the writer of Hebrews is endeavoring to convey to us, his readers. Its full context will be alive in our prayer life and throughout every aspect of our lives.
This is what Hebrews is trying to tell us:

We will understand the majesty and sovereignty of Jesus Christ.

We will understand our position in Him.

We will understand our relationship with our Heavenly Father.

We will understand entering His rest.

We will understand being part of a royal priesthood.

We will understand our Great High Priest.

We will understand being in the Holiest of Holies.

We will understand how God gets His rest in us.

We will understand Jesus compared to even the most remarkable human beings that have ever lived. They will all pale into insignificance compared to Him.

We will learn to hear from Him.

We will walk in awe and reverence that will humble our souls while oddly building confidence and assuredness at once.

We all struggle with prayer, and I am no exception. Nor am I an expert, either on prayer or relationships. God has simply allowed me to go through some precious trials and experiences, allowing me to write this book. He taught me how to handle these experiences and to share them with other saints–with *you*. Now, I'd like to look at an example of the kind of life and prayer I believe God had in mind for New Testament believers: Stephen.

Stephen

Stephen, the first martyr, is displayed in the narrative of the early church as an incredible example of how the character that God requires in us can be built by applying this prayer discipline in one's life.

In Acts 7:54, we come across an incident where the Jews rush upon Stephen and stone him to death. Let's contemplate this. How do you think he could do what he did? Acts 7:54-60 tells us:

> [54] When they heard these things they were cut to the heart, and they gnashed at him with their teeth. [55] But he, being full of the Holy Spirit, gazed into Heaven and saw the glory of God, and Jesus standing at the right hand of God, [56] and said, "Look! I see the heavens opened and the Son of Man standing at the right hand of God!" [57] Then they cried out with a loud voice, stopped their ears, and ran at him with one accord; [58] and they cast him out of the city and stoned him. And the witnesses laid down their clothes at the feet of a young man named Saul. [59] And they stoned Stephen as he was calling on God and saying, "Lord Jesus, receive my spirit." [60] Then he knelt and cried out with a loud voice, "Lord, do not charge them with this sin." And when he had said this, he fell asleep. (NKJV)

Stephen was not one of the apostles. He was one of the deacons put in charge of feeding the Hellenistic Jewish widows in Acts 6. But Stephen was full of the Spirit and preached wherever he went until he was put on trial for it. He boldly proclaimed the name of Jesus and was stoned to death by the enemies of Christ.

In the face of his immediate execution, Stephen simply placed himself out of the earthly situation and into the arms of Jesus. Furthermore, he acted like Jesus did when He was crucified on the cross, saying, "Lord, do not hold this sin against them."

Stephen had disciplined himself to be in this intimate relationship with Jesus through prayer. His relationship was an everyday part of his whole life. It was the place where he had found himself on so many occasions, so it was simple for him to go there again.

When Stephen preached his last sermon, he was full of the Spirit. This sermon had the power to save and the power to enrage the sons of the devil. Either way, Stephen was walking in the steps of his Lord, and his Lord was with and in him. Stephen was not even one of the twelve! Here is a model of the relationship that you and I can have with the Lord of all Creation if we go by faith in prayer regularly into the Holiest Place.

Stephen went home to be with his Lord even before they took his life. This takes a lot of hard work on one's knees. Sometimes we get to that Holy Place when we pray, and sometimes we don't. Sometimes it will come quickly, and sometimes it will take a lot of perseverance. *You just have to work through it until you arrive.*

Having done this the first time, it will come more readily; the more we discipline ourselves and persevere, the bolder and more confident we will get in reaching this goal.

SPIRITUAL RADAR

When we learn to pray in this manner, our spiritual radar will become so acute, so sensitive to His Being, that whenever even the slightest exaggeration threatens to proceed from our mouths, or the slightest wrong thinking attempts to enter our brains, this spiritual radar will start beeping like the seatbelt warning in your car when you forget to belt up. This warning happens because we are growing closer and closer to Him; therefore, His Purity shows the darkness that dwells within each of us.

Communion — Common Union

Just like the purpose of life in general, prayer is about oneness with God. To be in communion, Common Union with God, is to be at One with Him. We are merely specs of dust, but when we choose God, we become everything to Him.

Romans 12:1 tells us:

> *I beseech you therefore, brethren, by the mercies of God, that you present your bodies a living sacrifice, holy, acceptable to God, which is your reasonable service. (NKJV)*

> *I exhort you, therefore, brothers, in view of God's mercies, to offer yourselves as a sacrifice, living and set apart for God. This will please him; it is the logical "temple worship" for you*—CJB

Paul tells us in the Bible that we should pray without ceasing. I'm confident that most Christians think Paul is using hyperbole. But he is not. We *can* pray without ceasing in our daily lives. When we are in fellowship with Jesus, we are in a *state of prayer*. When we are with our families, at work, at home, at church, on holiday, or in the garden, we can be in communion with God. Words do not necessarily have to be coming out of our mouths. A life can be a life of prayer when lived in communion with God.

Can Communion Be Broken?

Can that communion be broken? If so, *How do we break that Common Union?* The answer is simple. *If we do something He cannot be part of, we break that Common Union when we push Him out of our lives.*

Where do we put God, Who lives inside us, when we gossip, lie, cheat, lust—when we switch on the internet, TV, telephone, and watch something we should not? We should ask ourselves this question: Where do we put God, Who inhabits His chosen vessels, while we indulge ourselves in these acts of sin? You can't take Him out and put Him on a shelf or under a blanket. You cannot say, "You wait over there, Lord, while I look at this pornography."

Paul says to walk by the Spirit, not the flesh. (Ro 8:1) This is what he means. We put on Christ and leave Him on, or we grieve His Holy Spirit and may as well not have Him at all. Prayer, in its essence, is union, and walking in holiness is prayer.

Let's reiterate what we have learned so far in this chapter.

HOW DO WE START OUR PRAYER?

Every day on our knees.

Matthew 11:28-30 says:

> [28] Come to Me, all you who labor and are heavy laden, and I will give you rest. [29] Take My yoke upon you and learn from Me, for I am gentle and lowly in heart, and you will find rest for your souls.

How does this register? This is GOD saying I am gentle and lowly in heart. One can spend hours on this alone. [30] "For My yoke is easy and My burden is light."

There is no easier place to be other than with Jesus; you can just relax and surrender to Him.

These verses are important, but it is also of supreme importance to comprehend and digest Verse 27 before those:

> All things have been delivered to Me by My Father, and no one knows the Son except the Father. Nor does anyone know the

Father except the Son, and the one to whom the Son wills to reveal Him.

When approaching God, we must start with relationship and not with things or objects that will all pass away upon His return. Becoming intimate with and knowing Father, Son, and Holy Spirit must precede everything else.

The previous sentence bears repeating: *Becoming intimate with and knowing Father, Son, and Holy Spirit must precede everything else.*

Start your prayers with adoration and meditate on just Who God is: His amazing, pure, holy, loving, righteous character and his fullness, richness, and beauty.

ENTER HIS REST

Psalms 100:4 says: "Enter into His gates with thanksgiving, And into His courts with praise. Be thankful to Him and bless His name."

Only then, from that place of peace and rest, can we put our petitions to Him correctly. It is so easy to pray in that state of rest because we are not struggling to be heard. We struggle to be heard because we have separated ourselves from Him through sin. God removes this hindrance when we rest in Him.
"In repentance and rest is your salvation. In quietness and trust is your strength." (Isa 30:15 NIV)

How Not to Pray

Most people come to Him when they need something or, by routine, throw everything that jumps into their minds at Him, then get off their knees (if they were on their knees) and walk away thinking to themselves, "Oh well that's done – ticked that box."

How many of our prayers are like this? How often do we throw a barrage of wants and needs straight at Him without ever first embracing Him in warm affection and love?

Imagine any other relationship we want to try to cultivate and maintain on this basis—wanting the relationship only for what we can get! How long would that relationship last?

Again, it is purely about union and relationship. Jesus wraps it all up in a few short words, and it cannot be said more clearly than this. John 17:3 says: "And this is eternal life, that they may know You, the only true God, and Jesus Christ Whom You have sent." It truly is nothing more than knowing God as a person with a heart, a personality, and an affection for you.

HOW, THEN, CAN WE PRAY WITHOUT CEASING?

1 Thessalonians 5:14-22 says: "Now we exhort you, brethren, warn those who are unruly, comfort the fainthearted, uphold the weak, be patient with all."

15v – *See that no one renders evil for evil to anyone, but continuously pursue what is good both for yourselves and for all.*
16v – *Rejoice always,*
17v – *pray without ceasing,*
18v – *in everything, give thanks; for this is the will of God in Christ Jesus for you.*
19v – *Do not quench the Spirit.*
20v – *Do not despise prophecies.*
21v – *Test all things; hold fast to what is good.*
22v – *Abstain from every form of evil.*

All these verses have their basis in verse 17 because a life of prayer in communion with God enables us to accomplish the other verses.

Paul would not have written this statement, "Pray without ceasing," if it was impossible. I believe it is possible to pray without ceasing if we have been filled with His Holy Spirit and living a life worthy of our calling in constant communion with God, not separating ourselves from Him by sin.

The Example of Marriage

To endeavor to explain this spiritual principle, we can look at a marriage. No matter what I am doing, either with my wife or without her, I am still married 24 hours a day, 365 days a year, and connected through the love that I have for my "one body" and the vows we took on our wedding day. I can only break that marriage by breaking my love or breaking my vows.

The Bible shows us that Jesus is the Groom, His bride is the Church, and that marriage between a man and a woman is genuinely about the mystery of Christ's marriage. Ephesians 5:28-32 says:

> [25] Husbands, love your wives, just as Christ also loved the Church and gave Himself for her, [26] That He might sanctify and cleanse her with the washing of water by the word, [27] That He might present her to Himself a glorious church, not having spot or wrinkle or any such thing, but that she should be holy and without blemish. [28] So, husbands ought to love their own wives as their own bodies; he who loves his wife loves himself. [29] For no one ever hated his own flesh, but nourishes and cherishes it, just as the Lord does the Church. [30] For we are members of His body, of His flesh, and of His bones. [31] "For this reason, a man shall leave his father and mother and be joined to his wife, and the two shall become one flesh." [32] **This is a great mystery, but I speak concerning Christ and the Church.**

JESUS is my first love, and HE is my betrothed; therefore, I would be unfaithful if I break my love or my vows. Faith and being faithful are the same—loyalty and staying loyal, and you can't say, "I have faith and yet be unfaithful." True *agape* love is based on trust; it is trusting in Him and Him being able to trust in us.

Consider the Song of Songs. It is, of course, a wonderful book about marriage and loving romance, but mystics and scholars have pointed to the book for centuries as the love story of God and Israel, God and Christ, and Christ and the Church.

Let's consider these relationships. Our human marriages contain the highest moments with the closest intimacy that can ever be humanly reached, beginning with "Adam knew his wife." (Ge 4)

More accurately, it started with, "This is now flesh of my flesh and bone of my bone." (Ge 2:23) Perhaps the only thing I can think of that would be more intimate than the love-making between a husband and wife is the consuming of the sacraments of the body and blood of our Lord.

Intimacy in the Mundane

There are those mountain-top moments of high romance in a marriage, for sure, but then there are the most mundane things, like doing the shopping, yard work, or having warmed-up leftovers together. There is sometimes tedious (but often wonderful) interaction with our children or even disciplining them. All of these are a part of the marriage relationship that never ceases.

The relationships are not broken in any of these occurrences. Just because, at times, we are doing the mundane, has the relationship ended? No, the marriage/relationship still stands. The intimacy and love remain. We are "married without ceasing."

If that is the reality in a marriage bond, why would we expect something different in our relationship with God? *Why are we led to believe that every prayer moment should be a pinnacle in our lives?* Marriage and sustaining the marriage can sometimes simply be hard work. Would it not make sense that the same could apply to a relationship with our Creator? Prayer can also be hard work and sharing time with God.

Going Through the Motions

In our prayer life, we can go through the motions and even think we are giving something to God, doing Him a favor. But adopt a different perspective: We are *"getting some of His valuable time!"*

We are getting One-on-one time with the Maker of all Creation, sometimes in the most intimate and deeply moving ways and other times in the simple, pure love of fellowship in the blessed mundane.

The Widow's Two Mites

> [1] And He looked up and saw the rich putting their gifts into the treasury, [2] And He saw also a certain poor widow putting in two mites. [3] So He said, "Truly I say to you that this poor widow has put in more than all; [4] for all these out of their abundance have put in offerings for God, but she out of her poverty put in all the livelihood that she had." (Lk 21:1-4 NKJV)

When Jesus pointed out the widow's offering, He showed that it wasn't what she had that mattered. It was that she gave all she had. Jesus' observation is usually preached as a sermon on giving. The application is never "give everything you have," but simply, "give a whole lot more than you are currently." But is that the point? I don't think the point is about money at all. It is about a heart. It is about the mundane. It is about a whole life.

We are each allocated only 24 hours daily—no more and no less. Will you ask yourself how much of that allocated time each day will you spend on God—living in His will, pleasing Him? "Spend wisely; spend eternally." What else is there?

I would like to give a few more examples:

Many of us attend a church meeting expecting a deep touch because we are singing, praising, praying, and listening to the Word of God preached. It can occasionally happen that we have an incredible encounter with Christ, receiving profound revelations, but this is not the norm, and to think it should be is misguided. I once attended such a meeting, and something more normal for me happened. I left the meeting, started the car, and then God touched me in the most dramatic and moving way from deep inside His Person.

You can be doing anything, and God will come and present Himself. He will intervene into a life when He sees an open and surrendered heart. God will surprise you in the mundane; you only have to be there with Him when it happens. This gift can happen as you open your eyes in the morning, and your first utterances will be praying in the Spirit in His languages, and God will drop straight into your spirit with what He would like to say to you.

Maybe He would have liked to have given what He wanted to share the night before, but we were too tired, or worse, we were full to the brim of the world's rubbish, *i.e.,* the internet, films, games, books, etc.

—*What you go to sleep with is nearly always what you will wake up with*—

Go to sleep with your wife, and you will wake up with your wife. The same is true of our relationship with God. Go to sleep with God, and you will wake up with God!

What are you thinking about in bed as you drift off to sleep? Are you watching television? What are you watching? Are you mindlessly scrolling, inviting the world and the evil one to dictate what you will process in your dreams?

Or are you praying? Are you thanking God for His mercies and blessing for that day? Are you confessing your sins and asking for His help for the next day and for your loved ones?

If you cannot discipline yourself concerning what you watch before bed, then at least give the final minutes to God, Who deserves much more. Then, when you wake up with God, your day will begin with you already abiding in Him.

God wants to visit with you. He wants constant connection, communion, and conversation with you, not just one way. In the next chapter, we will continue our discussion of prayer by specifically contemplating prayer with each member of the Godhead. If you continue with me in this meditation and genuinely seek to commune with God, your life will change dramatically, but it is crucial to understand this Triune God to Whom we cry out in loving prayer. In the next chapter, we will discuss the difference between praying to the Father, the Son, and the Holy Spirit and the childlike faith with which we must approach each.

CHAPTER 4:
PRAYER WITH THE FATHER, SON, AND HOLY SPIRIT

How Do We Get Back Relationship with God?

O ne of the aspects of prayer that will completely change how we pray is understanding Who we are praying to in our prayer life. My relationship with the Father is completely different from my relationship with Jesus, the Son, and my relationship with the Holy Spirit. Think back to all the sermons you've heard and books you've read; have you ever heard anyone teach on this subject? Yet, it is crucial to understand.

THE FATHER

God the Father is my heavenly Divine Father. Therefore, my prayer to Him is different from my prayer with Jesus and with the Holy Spirit. Look at how Jesus prayed to His Father in all His prayers on Earth, and you will see how we should approach the Father. This must be done with the most *reverence*, awe, and respect. He is so far above human comprehension. It is right to think of an earthly Father when trying to understand Him, but there are limits to this because we know no earthly fathers who are perfect and embody perfect holiness.

For example, I would defy anybody to define *infinite, omnipotent*/all-powerful, *omnipresent*/all in all, *seen and unseen, knowing simultaneously* every thought and every emotion in every human being that has ever lived or will live — ALL-KNOWING — ALL *AGAPE* LOVING — ALL PURE LIGHT.

Over and over in Scripture we are continually told about all the promises given only to those who fear God the Father. Jesus even said, "Do not fear him who can kill your body but fear Him Who can not only kill your body but can then also throw you into Hell, fear Him." (Lk 12:4-5)

We must never treat the Father with even the slightest disrespect or irreverence. This Psalm tells us the Father humbles Himself to look upon us His creation.

> [4] The Lord is high above all nations,
> His glory above the heavens.
> [5] Who is like the Lord our God,
> Who dwells on high,
> [6] Who humbles Himself to behold
> The things that are in the heavens and in the Earth?
> (Ps 113:4-6 NKJV)

Again, Jesus tells us that the Father is Spirit, and we must worship Him in spirit and truth.

> [23] But the hour is coming, and now is, when the true worshipers will worship the Father in spirit and truth; for the Father is seeking such to worship Him. [24] God is Spirit, and those who worship Him must worship in spirit and truth." (Jn 4:23-24 NKJV)

God the Father is beyond amazing because He has given us His creation. Being mere dust, we humans get to choose who our Father is, but we have only two choices that we can make in this regard.

We can choose our Heavenly Father, our Creator.

Or we can choose an earthly father, Satan, the father of lies.

There are no other choices. I have struggled for many years to understand and achieve the proper approach to the Father. I confess I held an inadequate understanding of Him until I spent the time meditating on these Words of Jesus. I then applied His Words in my life and went through Jesus to the Father. My respect and understanding transformed my relationship with *Abba* Father.

> [6]Jesus said to him, "I am the way, the truth, and the life. No one comes to the Father except through Me. [7] If you had known Me, you would have known My Father also; and from now on you know Him and have seen Him." (Jn 14:6-7 NKJV)

JESUS THE CHRIST - YESHUA MESSIAH

Where does one even start when we take into consideration all that Jesus Christ has done for us and continually does for us, how much He loved and goes on loving us, what He has given and goes on giving us? But we will attempt what we can according to God's revelation to us and let Christ do the rest; He will fill in all the blanks.

When we pray to the Son — Jesus, the One to Whom we are betrothed and will spend eternity married — we find our prayer with Him is entirely different from our prayer with the Father. I wrote briefly about this in the previous two chapters but read the following Scriptures for more insight into praying to and in partnership with our precious, pure Savior.

The Song of Songs is an imperative to understand the depth to which Jesus wants to take us in relationship.

Matthew 11:26-30
John 13 to 17
Psalm 22
Isaiah 52:13-15
Isaiah 53:1-12

If you read them, ask yourselves these following questions:

- Could I exist without Him?
- Could I be in Heaven if He were not there?
- Do I hunger and crave for His affections and company?
- Do I want to know every minute detail of His Person and personality?

To explore prayer to Jesus further, go back to the previous two chapters.

HOLY SPIRIT

The Holy Spirit is the One Who is preparing us, the Bride for the Groom; He is the Best Man. In Scripture, He is called:

- *RUACH HaKodesh*
- The ADVOCATE

- THE CONVICTOR of sin
- The COMFORTER our Strength
- The GIFT GIVER
- The Fruit BEARER
- The POWER
- The *CLETOS*

We find in the Scriptures one of the best examples of a best man in Genesis 24. This is a story about Abraham's servant, Eliezer, who was sent by Abraham back to his original homeland and to his nearest relatives to obtain a wife for his son Isaac. Abraham wanted a bride for the son God had given him from his tribe and people.

Eliezer was guided by the Hand of God straight to Rebekah, and then we know that he carefully partnered with God to recognize Rebekah. Then, when he knew 100% that she was the right girl, he brought her back prepared for her wedding to Isaac.

Now consider the parallels between Eliezer and the Holy Spirit in this account. The Holy Spirit sought us out, convicted us of sin, and pursued us to repentance, preparing us to come to our Savior.

The Holy Spirit is preparing us for Jesus through us handing our lives over to Him and giving Him sovereignty over all aspects of our lives, not just the ones we pick and choose.

If there is something in your life that is holding you back from reaching the full relationship and profound intimacy with Christ, that which He deserves from you, then you need to stop and go to the Holy Spirit and give Him full authority over that aspect of your life by completely surrendering it to Him. Give Him complete authority over the obstacle, whether pride, selfishness, timidity, or anything that is a blockage. Just give it to the Holy Spirit. He convicts you of sin and will give you the power and strength to overcome this and any affliction that besets your life and holds you back from reaching your fullness in Christ.

Therefore, when we pray to the Holy Spirit, we pray to Him to convict us and help us overcome. Those who are surrendered, submitted Saints walk under the authority of Jesus Christ and thus are entirely guided by His Holy Spirit. Our prayer life will be different and yet the same with all Three Persons of the Godhead.

Childlike Relationship with All of the Three

> [1] At that time, the disciples came to Jesus, saying, "Who then is greatest in the Kingdom of Heaven?" [2] Then Jesus called a little child to Him, set him in the midst of them, [3] and said, "Assuredly, I say to you, unless you are converted and become as little children, you will by no means enter the Kingdom of Heaven. [4] Therefore, whoever humbles himself as this little child is the greatest in the Kingdom of Heaven." (Mt18:1-4 NKJV)

Watch a child and carefully observe how she, through the stages of her growth, reacts with those she loves and trusts and those she is wary of. When children are young, you will see them snuggle deep into the necks of the ones they love or just sit beside them as they pull their arms across their faces to hide in those protective arms. Cup a child's face and watch him just lay his head over and feel the warmth of your hand. Stroke his forehead, and he will simply close his eyes in contentment and safety.

A wise man once told me this early in my Christian walk: If you want your child to relate to you when they grow up, you must relate to them when they are little. When they come to you with something they deem to be really important, stop and listen intently to what they want to say.

Don't push them away and say, "Not now; Daddy is too busy!" In later life, this will cost you dearly.

How have humans lost this simplicity in our lives? We have filled our lives with all the wrong junk, and we are teaching our children to be even worse than we are by handing them a mobile phone for their first birthday. Are we insane? What result do we expect to receive from this tragic mistake?

How do we get it back' There's only one way—*childlike faith*. We humble ourselves first and then pass this on to our children. Let them watch us approach God in a childlike manner, lifting our hands, palms facing up to Heaven, asking God for what we want.

Isn't this what a child does when they want something from their parents? "Please, Daddy," or "Please, Mommy." God requires a childlike response from us, and Jesus clearly tells us to come to the Father as a child.

Childlike Prayer

GOD loves childlike prayer. He loves the big "Why, Father?" when we approach God as a child and continually ask:

"Why have You written this like it is written in Your Word? Please help me to understand exactly what You are saying."
"When You were talking to these people, why did You talk in such a manner in the way You addressed them?"

"Why did You say this or do that?"

"What is this parable which is completely irrelevant to the situation right here in the middle of this passage of Scripture?"

Try this and see what happens. Be patient and wait to see how God will reveal His Word and Himself to you. It will amaze you, and you will derive such incredible joy doing what Jesus wanted when He said, "Come and learn from Me."

We have so many personal questions that there just don't seem to be answers to. For example, the tragic ones, like, "Why did my child have to pass away?" Or "Why did my mom have to die?"

He will always answer, and it will always be in His perfect timing. It may not be our timing, but it will be His. He knows our tomorrows; we don't! He also knows and understands us better than we know and understand ourselves. There are two great examples:

The first is in Luke 11. Here, the disciples ask Jesus to teach them to pray and how to speak to God the way He did. Looking at Luke 11:1-13, we might arrive at this question: Why did Jesus have this seemingly unrelated parable in the middle of answering the disciples' question, "*teach us to pray*"?

> [1] Now it came to pass, as He was praying in a certain place, when He ceased, *that* one of His disciples said to Him, "Lord, teach us to pray, as John also taught his disciples."
>
> [2] So He said to them, "When you pray, say:
>
>> Our Father in Heaven,
>> Hallowed be Your name.
>> Your kingdom come.
>> Your will be done
>> On Earth as *it is* in Heaven.
>> [3] Give us day by day our daily bread.
>> [4] And forgive us our sins,
>> For we also forgive everyone who is indebted to us.

> And do not lead us into temptation,
> But deliver us from the evil one."

⁵ And He said to them, "Which of you shall have a friend, and go to him at midnight and say to him, 'Friend, lend me three loaves; ⁶ for a friend of mine has come to me on his journey, and I have nothing to set before him'; ⁷ and he will answer from within and say, 'Do not trouble me; the door is now shut, and my children are with me in bed; I cannot rise and give to you'? ⁸ I say to you, though he will not rise and give to him because he is his friend, yet because of his persistence, he will rise and give him as many as he needs.

⁹ "So I say to you, ask, and it will be given to you; seek, and you will find; knock, and it will be opened to you. ¹⁰ For everyone who asks receives, and he who seeks finds, and to him who knocks it will be opened. ¹¹ If a son asks for bread from any father among you, will he give him a stone? Or if *he asks* for a fish, will he give him a serpent instead of a fish? ¹² Or if he asks for an egg, will he offer him a scorpion? ¹³ If you then, being evil, know how to give good gifts to your children, how much more will *your* Heavenly Father give the Holy Spirit to those who ask Him!" (Lk 11:1-13 NKJV)

In verses 5 to 8, Jesus answered the question of how to pray and also told them what to pray for: The Holy Spirit. And even more, how to receive Him by Knocking— Asking—Seeking continually until they receive Him.

This teaching also conveys here that Jesus is not teaching parrot prayer. He is not saying, "Do this prayer 10 times over in rote." Consider these initial words in verses 2-4. Each word is packed with the power of the universe. Read each few words, meditate, and pray on them one by one. You can easily spend 30-60 minutes meditating/praying on each line.

Luke 11:2-4:

> [2] And He said to them, "When you pray, say:

> Our Father in Heaven,

> Hallowed be your name.

> Your kingdom come,

> Your will be done, on Earth as *it is* in Heaven.

> [3] Give us each day our daily bread,

> [4] And forgive us our sins,
>   for we ourselves forgive everyone who is indebted to us.

> And lead us not into temptation,

> But deliver us from the evil one."

The second example is in the parable in Luke 18:1-8.

> [1] And He told them a parable to the effect that they ought always to pray and not lose heart. [2] He said, "In a certain city there was a judge who neither feared God nor respected man. [3] And there was a widow in that city who kept coming to him and saying, 'Give me justice against my adversary.' [4] For a while, he refused, but afterward he said to himself, 'Though I neither fear God nor respect man, [5] yet because this widow keeps bothering me, I will give her justice, so that she will not beat me down by her continual coming.'" [6] And the Lord said, "Hear what the unrighteous judge says. [7] And will not God give justice to his elect, who cry to him day and night? Will he delay long over them? [8] I tell you, he will give justice to them speedily. Nevertheless, when the Son of Man comes, will he find faith on Earth?"

Why does this parable of the unjust judge and the persistent woman end up with *"will I find faith on the Earth when I come back"*? Jesus tells us, His bride-to-be, "Never stop praying no matter your circumstances, no matter what happens, no matter how much this world falls into decay unraveling itself, whatever you see, keep connected, and keep praying."

> [8] I tell you, he will give justice to them speedily. Nevertheless, when the Son of Man comes, will he find faith on Earth?"

Childlike prayer should never cease in a Christian life. We will never have all the answers, but He does. He is perfection, He is pure.

No matter what comes upon this Earth, don't stop praying. Please don't fall for the heretical teaching of the pre-tribulation rapture; it is not true, even though I wish it were. We will all go through the great tribulation, and this tragic teaching and belief will be costly beyond measure when we enter that time. I believe this is precisely why Jesus gave us this warning.

REFLECTIONS

When we journey through our Bibles and look at some of the relationships and the simple prayers that men and women had with our Holy Father, we soon realize that God has always wanted a simple, yet deep intimate relationship with His creation. As I've been shouting throughout this book, *God wants a relationship, not a religion.*

Genesis 3: 8-11 says:

> [8] *And they heard the sound of the Lord God walking in the garden in the cool of the day, and Adam and his wife hid themselves from the presence of the Lord God among the trees of the garden.* [9] *Then the Lord God called to Adam and asked him, "Where are you?"* [10] *So he said, "I heard Your voice in the garden, and I was afraid because I was naked; and I hid*

myself." [11] *And He said, "Who told you that you were naked? Have you eaten from the tree of which I commanded you that you should not eat?"* (NKJV)

What was God's relationship to Adam and Eve here? What was their communion like? It was *simple*. It was *childlike*.

These few words paint the only picture we are given in all Scripture. So, we need to stand back and imagine the relaxed, normal relationship that they had with God. He was in complete union with them in everything they would have done daily; even in their most intimate moments, God hadn't moved off the scene nor hidden His face.

God designed these relationships and unions between a man and his wife. But man has come along and defiled, polluted, and corrupted what God had made so pure and perfect. God wanted a family that would be just like His Perfect Son. He wanted us to have His children so that He could enjoy them, and they could enjoy Him and love Him for Who He is. He has never changed and never wanted anything different than simply His image in us, His creation.

Moses and the Israelites

What Adam lost, Abraham's children could have gotten back, and there was no better time to restore this relationship than after God rescued His people from slavery in Egypt. In the Exodus, we have a detailed example of what God has always wanted, and the result can only be described as tragic.

Exodus 19:4-6:

> [4] "You have seen what I did to the Egyptians, and how I bore you on eagles' wings and brought you to Myself. [5] Now

therefore, if you will indeed obey My voice and keep My covenant, then you shall be a special treasure to Me above all people; for all the Earth is Mine. ⁶ And you shall be to Me a kingdom of priests and a holy nation. These are the words which you shall speak to the children of Israel." (NKJV)

Verse 9 tells us:

And the Lord said to Moses, "Behold, I come to you in the thick cloud, that the people may hear when I speak with you and believe you forever." (NKJV)

And then verses 16-17:

¹⁶ Then it came to pass on the third day, in the morning, that there were thunderings and lightnings, and a thick cloud on the mountain; and the sound of the trumpet was very loud so that all the people who were in the camp trembled. ¹⁷ And Moses brought the people out of the camp to meet with God, and they stood at the foot of the mountain. (NKJV)

Exodus 20:1-2:

¹ And God spoke all these words, saying, ² "I am the LORD your God, Who brought you out of the land of Egypt, out of the house of bondage." (NKJV)

Exodus 20:18-22:

¹⁸ Now all the people witnessed the thunderings, the lightning flashes, the sound of the trumpet, and the mountain smoking; and when the people saw it, they trembled and stood afar off. ¹⁹ Then they said to Moses, "You speak with us, and we will hear; but let not God speak with us, lest we die." ²⁰ And Moses said

> to the people, "Do not fear; for God has come to test you, and that His fear may be before you, so that you may not sin." [21] So the people stood afar off, but Moses drew near the thick darkness where God was. [22] Then the LORD said to Moses, "Thus you shall say to the children of Israel: You have seen that I have talked with you from Heaven."

What must God have thought about the Israelites' reaction to hearing His voice? God did all to display His Sovereignty over all creation by the great miracles HE performed to purchase this bride for Himself from the Egyptians. But now the Israelites want a man (Moses) between themselves and God, obliquely rejecting Him (and it won't be the last time). What must God have thought?

How incredible this is! But the truth is, it has never changed. Intimacy with God scares people for one reason or another. Intimacy requires commitment. People still like to have God at a distance so that they can remain in control of their lives.

God has always wanted to reveal Himself to us, dine with us, and have sweet communion with us. Something is wrong with us if we do not want the same things in our relationship with Him. That "something" has existed since the serpent in the garden. (Gen 3)

Exodus 24:1:

> Now, He said to Moses, "Come up to the LORD, you and Aaron, Nadab and Abihu, and seventy of the elders of Israel, and worship from afar."

Verses 9-12:

> [9] Then Moses went up, also Aaron, Nadab, and Abihu, and seventy of the elders of Israel, [10] and they saw the God of Israel.

And there was under His feet as it were a paved work of sapphire stone, and it was like the very heavens in its clarity. [11] But on the nobles of the children of Israel He did not lay His hand. So, they saw God, and they ate and drank.

These men dined with God. I believe that this was Jesus that the 74 men dined with; what an honor and a privilege to see God. This is what is intended for every child of God, nothing less. It was another occasion when the Son of God appeared to men. This would have been Jesus that they dined with; it had to be, as is explained below.

Look at the verses below at how Joshua stayed focused and would not risk losing any close connection with his Creator, no matter the cost to him personally. Here is a man after God's own heart. May we all be like this!

Exodus 33:11:

> So the LORD spoke to Moses face to face, as a man speaks to his friend. And he would return to the camp, but his servant, Joshua, the son of Nun, a young man, did not depart from the tabernacle (again, Jesus speaking face to face with Moses).

This is one of those instances where people will grab a single scripture without knowing the complete fullness of the Trinity and they will say 'There you go; the Bible contradicts itself'.

And he said, "Please, show me Your glory." Then He said, "I will make all My goodness pass before you, and I will proclaim the name of the Lord before you. I will be gracious to whom I will be gracious, and I will have compassion on whom I will have compassion." But He said, "You cannot see My face; for no man shall see Me, and live." And the Lord said, "Here is a place by Me, and you shall stand on the rock. So it shall be, while My glory passes by, that I will put you in the cleft of the rock and will cover you with My hand while I pass by. Then I will take away My hand, and you shall see My back; but My face shall not be seen."

Exodus 33:18-23 NKJV:

So, the explanation is for both Exodus 24:9-12 and Exodus 33:11 is that it was Jesus/God the Son Who presented Himself to the 74 men and spoke face to face with Moses.

Don't you just love this guy, Joshua? Even when Moses returned to the people, Joshua stayed at the tabernacle; he wasn't going anywhere or going to miss anything that the relationship with God would bring. Both times Moses went up and down the mountain, Joshua was there to meet him as he was coming down. What a man of God!

The Shining face of Moses

Exodus 34:29:

> Now it was so, when Moses came down from Mount Sinai (and the two tablets of the Testimony were in Moses' hand when he came down from the mountain), that Moses did not know that the skin of his face shone while he talked with Him.

Verses 33-35:

> And when Moses had finished speaking with them, he put a veil on his face. But whenever Moses went in before the LORD to speak with Him, he would take the veil off until he came out; and he would come out and speak to the children of Israel whatever he had been commanded. And whenever the children of Israel saw the face of Moses, that the skin of Moses' face

shone, then Moses would put the veil on his fa*ce again, until he went in to speak with Him.*

The Person Who Moses spoke face to face with would have been Jesus because of what we read in Exodus 33:18-23 where GOD clearly states that man cannot see the face of GOD and live. The Bible never contradicts itself; it is only if we apply the wrong application and human understanding and we do not know the Word of GOD sufficiently that it can appear to contradict itself.

How can a praying person be recognized? Such persons carry the glow of the presence of God about them. They will rarely speak about themselves, and when they do, it will nearly always be about an experience of what God has done in them or for them in their lives. "Out of the Abundance of the heart the mouth speaks." (Mt 12:34)

Let's get back to where we started at the beginning of this section. Jeremiah 31:31-34 says:

> [31] Behold, the days are coming, says the LORD, when I will make a new covenant with the house of Israel and with the house of Judah— [32] not according to the covenant that I made with their fathers in the day that I took them by the hand to lead them out of the land of Egypt, My covenant which they broke, though I was a husband to them, says the LORD. [33] But this is the covenant that I will make with the house of Israel after those days, says the LORD: "I will put My law in their minds, and write it on their hearts; and I will be their God, and they shall be My people. [34] No more shall every man teach his neighbor, and every man his brother, saying, 'know the LORD,' for they all shall know Me, from the least of them to the greatest of them, says the LORD."

For I will forgive their iniquity, and their sin I will remember no more.

The exact words of these Scriptures are repeated twice by the writer of the book of Hebrews in Chapters 8 and 10. Why is it repeated three times in our Bible? The reason is that this statement is referring to the blood covenant of Jesus Christ. This is the covenant of the internal, not external. Because of the price that has been paid to bring this new covenant, we share in it and enter straight into direct relationship in prayer with Jesus into the Holy of Holies. Hebrews 10:19-22 says:

> [19] Therefore, brethren, having boldness to enter the Holiest by the blood of Jesus, [20] by a new and living way which He consecrated for us, through the veil, that is, His flesh, [21] and having a High Priest over the house of God, [22] let us draw near with a true heart in full assurance of faith, having our hearts sprinkled from an evil conscience and our bodies washed with pure water.

Ephesians 2:4-7 says:

> [4] But God, Who is rich in mercy, because of His great love with which He loved us, [5] even when we were dead in trespasses, made us alive together with Christ (by grace you have been saved), [6] and raised us up together, and made us sit together in the heavenly places in Christ Jesus, [7] that in the ages to come He might show the exceeding riches of His grace in His kindness toward us in Christ Jesus.

This is where we are now seated with Christ Jesus in the heavenly places. We need to stop and see ourselves there.

WARNING ABOUT BOOKS AND TEACHING

Please, brothers and sisters! Be careful what you take in – what you read. Thousands of books have been written about God, the Bible, prayer, and the Holy of Holies. We can never know the true state of the person presenting to us. They may not be filled with the Holy Spirit; they may have absorbed so much bad teaching and are just passing on the errors they have learned. Or even worse, they could be conducting their lives in an ungodly way.

We don't need all this stuff that people are pumping out solely to make money and make a name for themselves; so much of it is man lifting man. But Jesus said, "If I be lifted up from the Earth, I will draw all men unto me." (Jn 12:32) Let's just spend our time, money, and energy to lift Jesus up for all the world to see.

James puts it all in simple terms in James 5:16:

> Confess your trespasses to one another, and pray for one another, that you may be healed. The effective, fervent prayer of a righteous man avails much.

Jude, the brother of our Lord, says:

Jude 1:20-21:

> But you, beloved, building yourselves up on your most holy faith, praying in the Holy Spirit, keep yourselves in the love of God, looking for the mercy of our Lord Jesus Christ unto eternal life.

THE WORD/JESUS AND PRAYER

Look at these few words as Jude has written them and the promises they bring When we pray in the Holy Spirit.

He...

1. Builds us up in our most holy faith.
2. Keeps us in the love of God.

3. Places us in a position to receive the mercy of God.
4. Brings eternal life.

This is our sufficiency.

Can a person pray without ceasing? I wrote about this earlier regarding living in intimacy with God, but now, let's take a different angle. I believe prayer without ceasing is possible with our beautiful Holy Spirit and His pure prayer language. Praying in other languages, no matter where we are or the situation, we can go directly to the Father, Son, and Holy Spirit with this divine new tongue that He has given us.

I will refrain from a thorough treatment of the gift of tongues here. But for those who neglect this gift, saying it was for Bible times but not today, I will ask you: What else is for Bible times but not today? Grace? Forgiveness? The Kingdom of God? Why would tongues pass away, but not other spiritual gifts? We must preach the Word, not only our experiences.

Prayer of Prayers

Let's finish this chapter with the "prayer of prayers," the prayer of Jesus. He wants us to pursue Him, not for what we can get, but for Who He is.

I hope you read John 17 earlier, as it is the one amazing prayer of our dear, sweet Lord Jesus. But even more impressive is that our Lord finishes His prayer by asking His Father to love us precisely in the same manner as the Father loves the Son!

Verse 23 - *I in them, and You in Me; that they may be made perfect in one, and that the world may know that You have sent Me, and have loved them as You have loved Me.*

<u>Verse 26</u> - *And I have declared to them Your name, and will declare it, that the love with which You loved Me may be in them, and I in them.*

Jesus asks not once but twice. How could the Father refuse this prayer for each one of us from His only Son?

To get the full impact of just what Jesus is asking His Father, again, we should read John Chapters 13 to 17. These wonderful chapters are the last will and testament of our Sweet Savior and are my favorite Scriptures in the entire Bible.

There is one final prayer which GOD WILL NOT REFUSE TO ANSWER: WHEN WE PRAY TO BE MORE LIKE HIS SON — CHANGED INTO HIS IMAGE. MAY WE DO SO AS LONG AS WE AWAIT HIS RETURN!

In the next chapter, we will discuss…

CHAPTER 5:

WHAT DOES IT TAKE TO MAKE GOD WEEP?

What Does It Take to Affect God and Why Has He Allowed Himself to be Vulnerable with Us?

Because we struggle so much to relate to God on a personal level—one of the most tragic realities of existence in a fallen world—it is difficult to grasp the emotional capacity of our God, Who the Bible tells us weeps for His children. It is hard to imagine ourselves having any effect whatsoever on God. At once, we are both prideful and self-centered, but deep down, we are self-loathing, struggling to grasp that we matter to anyone, let alone the God of all Creation. But we do.

In all of Scripture, we read only twice where Jesus wept. In those moments, humankind witnessed God crying. When we read these few words on both occasions, they tend to convey a picture of a stoic Jesus with a few tears running down His cheeks despite Himself. I do not believe this is what happened in those moments. I would like to endeavor to paint what I believe to be an accurate picture of what took place at these two events. As we look deeper at these episodes, I think you will come to the same conclusion.

My mother passed away several years ago, and tragically, she had rejected Jesus right up until the day of her death. The Lord has blessed me to lead and witness many people come to know and surrender to Him, but He did not grant my mother to be saved. It was her choice, but it was a bitter reality. As she wasted away, I had ample time to reflect and grieve. However, throughout the grieving process, I did not shed a tear right up until the moment when they lowered her into the grave. At that very instant, I dropped to my knees and wept convulsively, my chest and shoulders heaving with grief and tears streaming down my face in front of God and all the witnesses. The realization had finally hit home; my dear mother was going to spend eternity in Hell when she did not have to. This thought was so overwhelming it shattered me.

160,000 Per Day

There are 160,000 deaths in our world every day, and the vast majority of those deaths will result in that person passing and spending their eternity in Hell.

I believe that when Jesus wept, He went through the same set of circumstances that I had experienced by dropping to His knees in a similar manner. Further, I believe that the same thing happens to the Father, Son, and Holy Spirit *every time a human being dies without knowing Them.* I can't comprehend how, but I know God, so I know it is true. If even the angels rejoice when a lost sinner is found (Lk 15:10), how much more will the Godhead weep when one of His created image-bearers refuses the gift of life and instead opts for eternal torment and rejection?

147

GOD WANTS THE PERSON WITHIN EACH BODY–NOT THE BODY

We have the name Lazarus only twice in our Bibles. The first time the name is mentioned is in Luke 16 when Jesus tells the parable of the beggar Lazarus, and the other time is about Lazarus, the brother of Mary and Martha, who is the one that Jesus raised from the dead (Jn 11).

We also only read twice in our Bibles that Jesus wept. Once at the tomb of Lazarus, and the second time when He entered Jerusalem just before His crucifixion. There is a distinct correlation between the two facts. This is one of those occasions where we need to come as a child and ask Jesus, "What do You want to say; what teaching do You want us to understand?"

When we look at the timing of when Jesus gave the parable about the poor man Lazarus and the occasions of His weeping and why Jesus chose the use of this name for His parable when He could have chosen any other, then we go to our Lord and ask Him what is He saying to us, He provides us with His answer. His answer then allows us to see His deepest emotions. Luke 16:19-31 tells us:

> [19] There was a certain rich man who was clothed in purple and fine linen and fared sumptuously every day. [20] But there was a certain beggar named Lazarus, full of sores, who was laid at his gate, [21] desiring to be fed with the crumbs which fell from the rich man's table. Moreover, the dogs came and licked his sores. [22] So it was that the beggar died and was carried by the angels to Abraham's bosom. The rich man also died and was buried. [23] And being in torments in Hades, he lifted his eyes and saw Abraham afar off, and Lazarus in his bosom. [24] Then he cried and said, "Father Abraham, have mercy on me, and send Lazarus that he may dip the tip of his finger in water and cool my tongue; for I am tormented in this flame." [25] But Abraham

said, "Son, remember that in your lifetime you received your good things, and likewise Lazarus evil things; but now he is comforted and you are tormented. [26] And besides all this, between us and you there is a great gulf fixed, so that those who want to pass from here to you cannot, nor can those from there pass to us." [27] Then he said, "I beg you therefore, father, that you would send him to my father's house, [28] for I have five brothers, that he may testify to them, lest they also come to this place of torment." [29] Abraham said to him, "They have Moses and the prophets; let them hear them." [30] And he said, "No, Father Abraham; but if one goes to them from the dead, they will repent." [31] But he said to him, "If they do not hear Moses and the prophets, neither will they be persuaded though one rises from the dead."

In this passage of Scripture, Jesus provides us with a clear warning of Hell and all that comes with it. There is nowhere in our Bibles that is this descriptive of Hell and the torment of separation from God.

The timing of this parable in Luke 16 is crucial to help show the divinity of Christ even while He was here on Earth in His human flesh. Jesus gave this parable approximately six months before He raised Lazarus from the dead at Bethany. When telling this parable, why, of all the names available to Him, did Jesus choose to use this name, Lazarus? What is the significance of this name?

Was it not because He knew that He would raise a dead Lazarus back to life as is told in John 11?

Luke 17:11 says: "Now it happened as He went to Jerusalem that He passed through the midst of Samaria and Galilee."

I know I am repeating myself here, but the timing of when Jesus told this story of Hell is critical. We read that Jesus is coming through

Samaria and Galilee up to Jerusalem, so He provides this warning sometime before He raises Lazarus from the dead.

By selecting the name Lazarus, Jesus is telling everyone that He knows the future. Nothing is hidden from Him. (The only thing we know to be hidden from Him is the time of His return [Mt 24:36].) He knows that He will soon raise Lazarus from the dead, so He uses this name. This is also why He ends this parable in the manner He did. Verse 31 says: "They will not believe even if they see and hear from someone that has come back from the dead." It is their "hardness of heart" that grieves Him.

John 11:1-37 says:

> [1] Now a certain *man* was sick, Lazarus of Bethany, the town of Mary and her sister Martha. [2] It was *that* Mary who anointed the Lord with fragrant oil and wiped His feet with her hair, whose brother Lazarus was sick. [3] Therefore the sisters sent to Him, saying, "Lord, behold, he whom You love is sick."
>
> [4] When Jesus heard *that,* He said, "This sickness is not unto death, but for the glory of God, that the Son of God may be glorified through it."
>
> [5] Now Jesus loved Martha and her sister and Lazarus. [6] So, when He heard that he was sick, He stayed two more days in the place where He was. [7] Then after this He said to *the* disciples, "Let us go to Judea again."
>
> [8] *The* disciples said to Him, "Rabbi, lately the Jews sought to stone You, and are You going there again?"
>
> [9] Jesus answered, "Are there not twelve hours in the day? If anyone walks in the day, he does not stumble, because he sees the light of this world. [10] But if one walks in the night, he stumbles, because the light is not in him." [11] These things He

said, and after that He said to them, "Our friend Lazarus sleeps, but I go that I may wake him up."

[12] Then His disciples said, "Lord, if he sleeps, he will get well." [13] However, Jesus spoke of his death, but they thought that He was speaking about taking rest in sleep.

[14] Then Jesus said to them plainly, "Lazarus is dead. [15] And I am glad for your sakes that I was not there, that you may believe. Nevertheless, let us go to him."

[16] Then Thomas, who is called the Twin, said to his fellow disciples, "Let us also go, that we may die with Him."

I Am the Resurrection and the Life

[17] So when Jesus came, He found that he had already been in the tomb four days. [18] Now Bethany was near Jerusalem, about two miles away. [19] And many of the Jews had joined the women around Martha and Mary to comfort them concerning their brother.

[20] Then Martha, as soon as she heard that Jesus was coming, went and met Him, but Mary was sitting in the house. [21] Now Martha said to Jesus, "Lord, if You had been here, my brother would not have died. [22] But even now I know that whatever You ask of God, God will give You."

[23] Jesus said to her, "Your brother will rise again."

[24] Martha said to Him, "I know that he will rise again in the resurrection at the last day."

[25] Jesus said to her, "I am the resurrection and the life. He who believes in Me, though he may die, he shall live. [26] And whoever lives and believes in Me shall never die. Do you believe this?"

[27] She said to Him, "Yes, Lord, I believe that You are the Christ, the Son of God, Who is to come into the world."

[28] And when she had said these things, she went her way and secretly called Mary her sister, saying, "The Teacher has come and is calling for you." [29] As soon as she heard *that,* she arose quickly and came to Him. [30] Now Jesus had not yet come into the town but was in the place where Martha met Him. [31] Then the Jews who were with her in the house, and comforting her, when they saw that Mary rose up quickly and went out, followed her, saying, "She is going to the tomb to weep there."

[32] Then, when Mary came where Jesus was, and saw Him, she fell at His feet, saying to Him, "Lord, if You had been here, my brother would not have died."

[33] Therefore, when Jesus saw her weeping, and the Jews who came with her weeping, He groaned in the spirit and was troubled. [34] And He said, "Where have you laid him?"

They said to Him, "Lord, come and see."

[35] Jesus wept. [36] Then the Jews said, "See how He loved him!"

[37] And some of them said, "Could not this Man, Who opened the eyes of the blind, also have kept this man from dying?"

This account of Lazarus being sick, then dying and entombed for four days has raised many questions. I believe without doubt that the main question we all need to ask ourselves is, *what is the complete teaching that Jesus wants to get into our spirits through these Scriptures?*

What made Jesus weep loudly, audibly, not as we imagine a tear or two rolling down His cheek? This display would have been such that all present would have witnessed this deepest of human emotions in the same way the attendees of my mother's graveside memorial saw reality catch up to my heart as my mother's body was lowered into the cold ground, her soul already in Hell.

Why did Jesus allow Lazarus to die when He could have simply spoken a word and healed him?

To answer the question, we must only reflect on when Jesus healed the Centurion's servant from a distance. Why did He wait until he was in the grave for four days? Why did He not heal Lazarus from a distance? Jesus shows us in verses 4-6:

> [4] When Jesus heard that, He said, "This sickness is not unto death, but for the glory of God, that the Son of God may be glorified through it." [5] Now Jesus loved Martha and her sister and Lazarus. [6] So, when He heard that he was sick, He stayed two more days in the place where He was.

This whole event is orchestrated to glorify God and help us understand the impact we can have on Him personally. The Scriptures tell us how much Jesus loved this family. But verse 6 tells us that when He heard Lazarus was sick, He waited two more days. We suffer from poor human judgment, so we immediately assume if you love someone, you jump straight up and run to their aid when they are experiencing trouble. This is because we limit our thinking to the here and now, to this world and not the next eternal world. Jesus embodies an eternal perspective.

Verses 14-15 tell that Jesus states Lazarus is dead, and for their sakes, it was good that He was not there "that you may believe."

When Jesus arrived, seeing Mary in her bereaved state and those with her, many readers assume He wept out of sympathy for them. But did He weep for them? The answer is simply "no." He did not. He is here groaning and troubled on display for all to see; picture His face twisted, His body tensing in anguish, pulling back because of what He knew was going to happen after He raised Lazarus from death. "He groaned in the spirit and was troubled."

Verse 35 is the shortest verse in our Bibles: "Jesus wept."

So many have tried to answer this question of what made God weep. To answer, we must look at it all from an eternal perspective and in the context of how Jesus saw it all, knowing what will play out, not only this day but very soon.

Verses 36 to 46 say: "Then the Jews said see how He loved him!" And some said, "Could not this Man, Who opened the eyes of the blind, also have kept this man from dying?"

Verse 38: "Then Jesus, again groaning in Himself, came to the tomb. It was a cave, and a stone lay against it."

Again, picture what is happening to Jesus. Jesus is again groaning within Himself; He is in spiritual agony. Here, the God of the Universe is experiencing agony. Verse 45 tells us the good news that some believed: "Then many of the Jews who had come to Mary, and had seen the things Jesus did, believed in Him."

Here is the key to the answer to the question of what is causing the weeping, the groaning, the troubling in spirit, and all the anguish our Lord is suffering: Verse 46 tells us: "But some of them went away to the Pharisees and told them the things Jesus did."

Some believed, but others immediately set out to betray Him. It is almost impossible for us to believe after what they have just witnessed: someone dead four days sealed in a tomb got up and walked out!

What hardness of heart! How could you begin to comprehend this? But reflect on your walk with Jesus. Remember how quickly even a Christian heart can harden. How often have we encountered those who once believed what we believe but have become so hard and callous toward Christ?

There is a dire warning here: This hardness can come so fast that even if we miss one day with Jesus, we can often struggle to get back to that place of softness and closeness, being molded back into His image. Once turning to walk by the flesh, it can be difficult to turn back to walk by the Spirit.

There is a saying that I love and know to be true, "I need to be connected with Christ at least every 30 minutes every day so that my heart does not harden." I wholeheartedly agree with this statement.

John 11:47-53 tells us:

> [47] Then the chief priests and the Pharisees gathered a council and said, "What shall we do? For this Man works many signs. [48] If we let Him alone like this, everyone will believe in Him, and the Romans will come and take away both our place and nation." [49] And one of them, Caiaphas, being high priest that year, said to them, "You know nothing at all, [50] nor do you consider that it is expedient for us that one man should die for the people, and not that the whole nation should perish." [51] Now this he did not say on his own authority; but being high priest that year he prophesied that Jesus would die for the nation, [52] and not for that nation only, but also that He would gather together in one the children of God who were scattered abroad. [53] Then, from that day on, they plotted to put Him to death."

These evil men not only wanted to kill Jesus, but they also wanted to kill Lazarus because he was the living evidence that Jesus was God. The next verse shows us the timing of this event, well after the giving of the parable of Lazarus and the rich man in Hell. "And the Passover of the

CHRISTIANITY IS NOT A RELIGION. IT IS RELATIONSHIP

Jews was near, and many went from the country up to Jerusalem before the Passover, to purify themselves." (55)

That is the first account of the weeping Christ. He weeps because of their hardness of heart. The second account of Jesus weeping is even more straightforward and corroborates this idea.

Luke 19:37-44 tells us:

> [37] Then, as He was now drawing near the descent of the Mount of Olives, the whole multitude of the disciples began to rejoice and praise God with a loud voice for all the mighty works they had seen, [38] saying: "Blessed is the King Who comes in the name of the Lord!' Peace in Heaven and glory in the highest!" [39] And some of the Pharisees called to Him from the crowd, "Teacher, rebuke Your disciples." [40] But He answered and said to them, "I tell you that if these should keep silent, the stones would immediately cry out." [41] Now as He drew near, He saw the city and wept over it, [42] saying, "If you had known, even you, especially in this your day, the things that make for your peace! But now they are hidden from your eyes. [43] For days will come upon you when your enemies build an embankment around you, surround you and close you in on every side, [44] and level you, and your children within you, to the ground; and they will not leave in you one stone upon another, because you did not know the time of your visitation."

JESUS WEEPS A SECOND TIME

Jesus is weeping again. Why? He is weeping because within days, they would see the Son of God crucified and come back from the dead and still will not humble themselves and believe. Why are so many hearts so hard? Again, we should not think one or two tears slowly dripped down His cheek. He would have wept visibly and loudly as He heaved in agony. Even after Jesus was raised from the dead and appeared to over 500 brethren at once (1 Cor 15:6), their hearts would be hard.

We have been provided with so much undeniable evidence of everything He was and said and did—indisputable evidence of everything He claimed to be. I don't believe that there is such a thing as an atheist. There are only those who have different degrees of hatred for the One True God and His only begotten Son.

We are told that when Jesus died, He died of a broken heart.

From the Azusa Pacific University:

> The decreased oxygen (due to the difficulty in exhaling) causes damage to the tissues and the capillaries begin leaking watery fluid from the blood into the tissues. This results in a build-up of fluid around the heart (pericardial effusion) and lungs (pleural effusion). The collapsing lungs, failing heart, dehydration, and the inability to get sufficient oxygen to the tissues essentially suffocate the victim. § The decreased oxygen also damages the heart itself (myocardial infarction), which leads to cardiac arrest. In severe cases of cardiac stress, the heart can even burst, a process known as cardiac rupture. Jesus most likely died of a heart attack.

John 19:32-35 says:

> [32] Then the soldiers came and broke the legs of the first and of the other who was crucified with Him. [33] But when they came to Jesus and saw that He was already dead, they did not break His legs. [34] But one of the soldiers pierced His side with a spear, and immediately blood and water came out. [35] And he who has seen has testified, and his testimony is true; and he knows that he is telling the truth, so that you may believe.

So why are there only two times in our Bibles that the name of Lazarus appears, and why do we have the two occasions of Jesus weeping? They are both interconnected. God is trying to speak to us at every turn, and we just will not listen.

The role of telling human beings about Hell and an eternity of wailing and gnashing of teeth was solely left upon the shoulders of Christ Jesus to warn us to flee for our eternal life from this horrific future facing humanity.

"What makes GOD CRY? ROCK HARD HEARTS!"

The staggering fact that we can have this much impact on the Infinite Creator of Heaven and Earth and make Him cry is hard to fathom. This is just the start of the list of ways Jesus has revealed to us about Himself and His feelings and emotions toward us.

Let's look at more ways we impact and affect God and how He feels about us when we undertake certain things. Some interactions with Him bring Him great pleasure and enjoyment, but some things we do only bring Him torment and pain. We will start with the positive because this is what Jesus did when He wrote to the seven churches in Asia (Rev 1-3).

Zephaniah 3:17:

> "The Lord your God in your midst, the Mighty One, will save; He will rejoice over you with gladness. He will quiet you with His love, He will rejoice over you with singing."

Can you imagine this: the infinite God singing about His children with a great smile on His face? He has always been in the restoration business and is quick to bring back into His Family. We need to look no further than the Israelites to affirm this.

Zechariah 10:6-8:

> [6] I will strengthen the house of Judah, And I will save the house of Joseph. I will bring them back because I have mercy on them. They shall be as though I had not cast them aside; For I am the Lord their God, And I will hear them. [7] Those of Ephraim shall be like a mighty man, And their heart shall rejoice as if with wine. Yes, their children shall see it and be glad; Their heart shall rejoice in the Lord. [8] I will whistle for them and gather them, For I will redeem them; And they shall increase as they once increased.
> (An interesting note: God whistles three times in our Bibles here in Zechariah and twice in Isaiah)

Look through your Bibles at His endless promises to love, nurture, protect, and care for those who fear Him. We can grieve His Holy Spirit when we resist Him through our rebellion to His Person. Acts 7:51-53 says:

> [51] You stiff-necked and uncircumcised in heart and ears! You always resist the Holy Spirit; as your fathers did, so do you. [52] Which of the prophets did your fathers not persecute? And they killed those who foretold the coming of the just One, of whom you now have become the betrayers and murderers, [53] who have received the law by the direction of angels and have not kept it.

Ephesians 4:30 says:

"And do not grieve the Holy Spirit of God, by Whom you were sealed for the day of redemption."

Psalms 78:39-41 adds:

> [39] For he remembered that they were but flesh, A breath that passes away and does not come again. [40] How often they

provoked Him in the wilderness and grieved Him in the desert! [41] Yes, again and again they tempted God, and limited the Holy One of Israel.

GOD HAS ALLOWED HIMSELF TO BE VULNERABLE TO US HIS CREATED BEINGS, HE HAS PUT LAWS IN PLACE SUBJECTING HIS SOVEREIGNTY TO A PART OF HIS CREATION.

This is just so far above human understanding and is in fact overwhelming when contemplated.

We can thoughtlessly hurt Him through our actions and speech, trampling on His heart and forsaking Him as our Father and Creator. We all understand what it is like to grieve. Most of us have lost a close friend or a relative, and those losses take us through a process of mourning and grief. Why would it be any different for God, Who experiences loss every day? The following is a selection of verses that show God declaring His feelings toward His firstborn Israel.

In the book of Hosea, we have the most tender, affectionate display of how God loves and cares for His firstborn, Israel. We Christians have entered that same blood covenant with Israel, so He now feels the same way about us as He does about His firstborn. Through His *agape* love, He has rescued us from ourselves, from self-destruction and self-mutilation. Yet, we are unfaithful.

Hosea 2:16, 19-20, and 23 tell us:

> [16] "And it shall be, in that day," says the Lord, "That you will call Me 'My Husband', And no longer call Me 'My Master;' [19] I will betroth you to Me forever; Yes, I will betroth you to Me in righteousness and justice, In loving kindness and mercy; [20] I will betroth you to Me in faithfulness, And you shall know the Lord.

[23] "Then I will sow her for Myself in the Earth, And I will have mercy on her who had not obtained mercy; Then I will say to those who were not My people, 'You are My people!' And they shall say, 'You are my GOD'".

Hosea 11:1, 3-4, 7-9 says:

[1] When Israel was a child, I loved him, And out of Egypt I called My son.

[3] I taught Ephraim to walk, Taking them by their arms; But they did not know that I healed them. [4] I drew them with gentle cords, With bands of love, And I was to them as those who take the yoke from their neck. I stooped and fed them.

[7] My people are bent on backsliding from Me. Though they call to the Most High, None at all exalt Him. [8] "How can I give you up, Ephraim? How can I hand you over, Israel? How can I make you like Admah? How can I set you like Zeboiim? My heart churns within Me; My sympathy is stirred. [9] I will not execute the fierceness of My anger; I will not again destroy Ephraim. For I am God, and not man, the Holy One in your midst; And I will not come with terror.

God holds nothing back in these Scriptures. He opens His chest and bears His heart for all to see, humbling Himself beyond measure or comprehension.

In Matthew 11, Jesus said: "For I am Gentle and Lowly in heart."

Reading through John 17, one sees that Christ invites us all in to share with the Father, Son, and Holy Spirit the deepest, most intimate conversation between a Father and Son ever recorded. Jesus goes on to display the most selfless communication ever uttered. His prayer with His Father is so transparent of His inner Being that we get the honor of sharing the intimacy from the inside of not only Jesus but also His Father.

² As You have given Him authority over all flesh, that He should give eternal life to as many as You have given Him. ³ And this is eternal life, that they may know You, the only true God, and Jesus Christ Whom You have sent. ⁴ I have glorified You on the Earth. I have finished the work which You have given Me to do.

Jesus is saying, "I have displayed to them and to the world the incredible, Amazing Being that You are Father so that it is undeniable Who You are and Who I Am, the Son that You sent."

⁶ I have manifested Your name to the men whom You have given Me out of the world. They were Yours, You gave them to Me, and they have kept Your word. ⁷ Now they have known that all things which You have given Me are from You. ⁸ For I have given to them the words which You have given Me; and they have received them, and have known surely that I came forth from You; and they have believed that You sent Me.

In verses 9-11, Jesus prays for this closeness that He shares with His Father to be in each of us, with nothing of our relationship left out or lost.

⁹ I pray for them. I do not pray for the world but for those whom You have given Me, for they are Yours. ¹⁰ And all Mine are Yours, and Yours are Mine, and I am glorified in them. ¹¹ Now I am no longer in the world, but these are in the world, and I come to You. Holy Father, keep through Your name those whom You have given Me, that they may be one as We are.

Then in 20-21, He says:

²⁰ I do not pray for these alone, but also for those who will believe in Me through their word; ²¹ that they all may be one, as

> You, Father, are in Me, and I in You; that they also may be one
> in Us, that the world may believe that You sent Me.

Then, JESUS thrusts the bar to unprecedented levels of love for us by
entreating His Father, finishing this prayer with these majestic requests
by asking the Father that He would love us in the *same way He* loves
Him. Jesus not only puts forth this request once but also repeats the
prayer twice.

> [23] I in them, and You in Me; that they may be made perfect in
> one, and that the world may know that You have sent Me, and
> have loved them as You have loved Me.
>
> [26] And I have declared to them Your name, and will declare it,
> that the love with which You loved Me may be in them, and I
> in them.

As we have considered these emotions of God, we have observed the
makeup of the depth of relationship He has always had in His plan for
eternity. God, knowing all things and foreknowing that we silly humans
would put up every roadblock and diversion possible to His plan, has
established a process throughout history so that He can achieve His
final eternal result.

The Redemptive Story of Intimacy with God

Starting in the Garden of Eden, we can follow the relationship between
the Infinite Spirit and His creation and observe how these relationships
build one upon another as we read through the Scriptures.

The first relationship with Adam and Eve was special: walking in the
garden, communion between the Divine Being and beings of flesh. In
this situation, I believe Jesus was there because we see the first
references in Genesis to God as Being referred to by the Name of
ELOHIM (plural - two or more).

That relationship was not close enough or intimate enough for the Sovereign Maker. The closeness required was not there, and now we have lived with the consequences for more than 6,000 years. Had it been there, we would not have seen the first humans so vulnerable to Satan. Yet, this very fall will lead to the kind of intimacy with God we are speaking of.

Then we have Abraham, called the "Friend of God," who met and shared a meal with God as he spoke with and even dared to petition God. This was another appearance of Jesus. This relationship of *Phileo* (brotherly) love is still short of what God wants or expects for an eternal *agape* relationship. Please understand I don't want to detract from these amazing relationships; I often try to put myself in the place of people like Abraham and fail miserably. What I am saying, though, is God desires and offers so much more for our eternal Being together than what those men experienced, and this is a glorious truth that to miss is to invite the tragedy of failing to walk in the intimacy with God what we were created for.

We move on to Moses, the man to whom God spoke with, face to face on a continual daily basis. Again, this would have been Jesus, at least whenever He manifested in physical form (as He did to Joshua as the Captain of the Lord's Armies).
Then we have David, who was a man after God's own heart. (Acts 13:22)

> And when He had removed him, He raised up for them David as king, to whom also He gave testimony and said, 'I have found David the son of Jesse, a man after My own heart, who will do all My will.'

We get significant insight into the heart of God and David when we read the account in 2 Samuel after David had sinned with Bathsheba and murdered her husband, Uriah the Hittite, to cover his multitude of transgressions. Nathan, the prophet and friend of David, came to rebuke him because of what David had done.

> [1] Then the LORD sent Nathan to David. And he came to him and said to him, "There were two men in one city, one rich and the other poor. [2] The rich *man* had exceedingly many flocks and herds. [3] But the poor *man* had nothing, except one little ewe lamb which he had bought and nourished; and it grew up together with him and with his children. It ate of his own food and drank from his own cup and lay in his bosom; and it was like a daughter to him. [4] And a traveler came to the rich man, who refused to take from his own flock and from his own herd to prepare one for the wayfaring man who had come to him; but he took the poor man's lamb and prepared it for the man who had come to him." (2 Sam 12:1-4)

Why did Nathan put before the King the story of the poor man with the one lone sheep? Ask Jesus, and He will give the full story about David's heart. This is one of those examples of why we must come as children simply admitting to God, "We don't know, but You do, Father." We humble ourselves before the throne of Grace and ask, "Why?"

Remember David was a shepherd, then ask yourself, "Who is the Great Shepherd?"

There are many profound lessons for all of us in this story of relationship. When we read Scriptures like these, they point to lessons for our lives and relationships. It is vital to our well-being to change places from the human perspective and see things from God's heart and perspective.

God also said through Nathan to David, "I have given you wives and concubines, and also I would have given you much more." He gave so much to David, but David just wanted that one more thing that was not his to have. This is our fallen state.

How do you measure how much to give someone that you love? Think of your children. How do you give it all without spoiling your relationship or child?

Then, as we go again and read in John 17, we come to God's ultimate display of love and intimacy by giving His Son, our Lord Jesus Christ, so that we could experience God with all our senses.

God Himself lived with man for 33.5 years, and there was nothing of His character, nature, or person that He held back. Finally, man and his world could see, touch, hear, smell, and even taste God in His Fullness. But this was still not close enough for God and His children because the flesh will always fail and let Him down.

No, we move on to the closest relationship possible while we live in these earthen tabernacle/tents, where we get to be even closer to Jesus, His Father, and His Holy Spirit because He has ascended to be at the right hand of His Father. This is what He told His apostles must take place so He could send back the Holy Spirit to live within us earthen vessels. (Jn 14-16)

Can you imagine anything closer in a relationship than the Holy Spirit bringing the Father and the Holy Spirit to dwell inside your human body? There is no closer relationship than this to experience in this present age, that is, the age of human flesh.

And yet, this is *still* not close enough for God! Jesus Himself is pining for the day when He can share all that He is and all that He has with His bride. Luke 12:49-51 says:

> [49] I came to send fire on the Earth, and how I wish it were already kindled! [50] But I have a baptism to be baptized with, and

how distressed I am till it is accomplished! [51] Do you suppose that I came to give peace on Earth? I tell you, not at all, but rather division.

You will never hear these Scriptures preached on because we have become men-pleasers, but they show how Jesus is hungering and wanting us to hunger for the day when nothing comes between us and Him—the day when "the flesh" no longer can separate us.

Mutilation

He does not want the flesh and its failings and shortcomings coming between us. The flesh will create times of separation between ourselves and God through sin, which the flesh invites and allows it to come in. In a later chapter, we will explore fully the only acceptable (eventual) state of being that will be satisfactory for God's great love for His children. It grieves me when I write of the riches and beauty held in Christ and then must pen what we have done and continue to do to this precious gift of this most complex planet with all its splendors. It is nothing short of mutilation.

When we mutilate our bodies through sin, we must ask why we have chosen to do this to ourselves. What are we saying to ourselves when we do the following things to our bodies? What are we doing when we hate the body He gave us or when we are so full of ourselves that we say, "I can improve on what God has made."

We cover ourselves with tattoos, pierce our bodies in every conceivable place, stretch our earlobes to the point of deforming ourselves beyond repair, and abuse our bodies so they can no longer be recognized for their God-given gender. In short, we have elected to become grotesque. We may paint the outside with makeup and plastic surgery, but the real person living inside the body has become ugly and disgusting, shriveled up and dying by cutting itself off from the Very Source of all life.

If people stop and take time out from their self-consuming lives and just look at God with the desire to start a relationship, they will immediately find they will start falling in love with Him. He is so easy to be with.

> [28] Come to Me, all *you* who labor and are heavy laden, and I will give you rest. [29] Take My yoke upon you and learn from Me, for I am gentle and lowly in heart, and you will find rest for your souls. [30] For My yoke *is* easy and My burden is light." (Mt 11:28-30)

Jesus refers to Himself as "gentle and lowly in heart." He invites you to come into His residence and make your home with the easiest person on Earth to live with.

Remember, this is God speaking, Who is the Infinite Being speaking about Himself in this most humble way. We can stop failing miserably in our lives; there is an answer, and it is right in front of us. What makes God weep? He weeps when we reject the answer.

CHAPTER 6:
HOW DO I GET BACK INTO THE FATHER'S KINGDOM?

How Do I Repent and Turn Back to Him?

Jesus Christ came preaching the Kingdom of God. He announced that it had come and was coming. He demonstrated its presence by manifesting kingdom reality all around Him. In the kingdom, there is no sickness—He drove out sickness. In the kingdom, demons are not allowed to torment humanity—demons screamed in their torment when Jesus came around. In the kingdom, there is no death, there is no unsatisfied hunger, there is no unforgiveness—Jesus' prayer, "Let your kingdom come," was not mere words, but light and life manifested amid the darkness of fallen creation, showing that not only was God's Kingdom coming, but it had been inaugurated. Ever since, the believer's work has been to "seek first the Kingdom of God" (Mt 6:33) and allow God to add unto it what He will. To be a disciple of Jesus is to get into God's Kingdom and stay in God's Kingdom. The problem with the Church today? Many of us have not sought the kingdom and have taken up residence in the dominion of darkness instead. We must come back in.

Of first importance is to answer the question: Into whose kingdom do we want to be invited? Let us make sure we know and love the King of this kingdom even more than the kingdom itself.

In short, it is God's Kingdom. This is the God I have tried with all my might to describe throughout this book, especially in Chapter 1. He is our Maker, Lord, Savior, Lover of our Soul, Husband, Father, the Object of our most reverent worship. Our King.

Therefore, it is He, and He alone, Who has made the rules for entering His own kingdom. We cannot rudely crash the gates with our own set of rules and say, "Well, I have arrived! Now, where is my spot?" That is not how it works. We humans must stop pretending we are gods and that we make up the rules. We need to grow up and stop acting like babies every time God provides us with a precise way to live our lives harmoniously on Earth and, more importantly, eternally with Him. Why, like rebellious teenagers, do we always think we know better when the simple answers are always given to us?

You Must Be Born Again

We need to look no further than the careful instructions given to Nicodemus and to us by Jesus. He told the Pharisee who came by night the conditions by which a man or a woman must enter and be a part of His Kingdom. The record is in John 3:3-6:

> [3] Jesus answered and said to him, "Most assuredly, I say to you, unless one is born again, he cannot see the Kingdom of God." [4] Nicodemus said to Him, "How can a man be born when he is old? Can he enter a second time into his mother's womb and be born?" [5] Jesus answered, "Most assuredly, I say to you, unless one is born of water and the Spirit, he cannot enter the

Kingdom of God. ⁶That which is born of the flesh is flesh, and that which is born of the Spirit is spirit.

The Complete Jewish Bible puts it like this: JESUS could not make it any less complicated:

> "Yes, indeed," Yeshua answered him, "I tell you that unless a person is born again from above, he cannot see the Kingdom of God." Nakdimon said to him, "How can a grown man be 'born'? Can he go back into his mother's womb and be born a second time?" YESHUA answered, "Yes, indeed, I tell you that unless a person is born from water and the Spirit, he cannot enter the Kingdom of God. What is born from the flesh is flesh, and what is born from the Spirit is spirit." Yochanan (John) 3:3-6 CJB

It is simple, but while this is true, it requires a humbling of oneself and complete surrender to the will of God. Our problem is we don't like anyone telling us what to do, even, and especially God. How foolish we are when He has made it so uncomplicated and easy. Here are the simple steps:

First, we must be "born of the water." We must receive baptism.

Then, or simultaneously, we must be born from above of the Holy Spirit.

These two simple commandments from Jesus, combined with the practice of repentance and belief, bring us into His Kingdom. All these steps of obedience can happen in a day or a moment, but because we are so stiff-necked in rebellion, it normally takes longer.

We must remember that John, who wrote this gospel, was a simple fisherman, and he would not have penned his gospel in complex Greek;

he would have written it in either Aramaic or Hebrew, as much of the New Testament was also written.

Can we imagine Matthew wrote his gospel, which is the gospel to the Jews, in Greek? Or that the book to the Hebrews was written in Greek? Or would James (the brother of Jesus) write his epistle to the twelve tribes scattered abroad in Greek? It is highly unlikely. Therefore, we must read this with the understanding they would have originally been written in Hebrew or Aramaic, which changes the meaning somewhat. It doesn't change it so much that we should question the validity of the Bible, but we should be aware of where the nuance is altered slightly because of the difference in how the languages work.

In the Jewish understanding of the writing in John 3, the words "born again" are not there.

There are only the words "born from above." When we know that and we read this passage, it makes complete sense.

Jesus reaffirms these simple-to-follow commandments in John 4:23-24:

> [23] "But the hour is coming, and now is, when the true worshipers will worship the Father in spirit and truth; for the Father is seeking such to worship Him. [24] God is Spirit, and those who worship Him must worship in spirit and truth."

We need to note the word "must" here. There are no other options. Our relationship with all Three Persons must be in His Spirit and His Truth, not *our* spirit and *our* truth.

Four basic commands are given in this passage, which are steps we all need to obey to enter the Kingdom of God. These four steps are clearly defined first by the Lord Jesus Christ and then reaffirmed throughout the New Testament by the apostles.

These are:

1. Repent - Turn from your sins.

2. Believe in Jesus the Christ. That is, trust in and rely on Him and obey Him.

3. Be baptized by full immersion in water.

4. Receive the Holy Spirit as He is irrefutably given to us (shown in Acts 2, 8, 10-11, and 19).

Christianity was originally called "the Way," and we Christians are all on this journey of being on the way. While we may have reached one stage, we should not believe we have arrived. Jesus is calling us on, and that calling will not cease until we pass from this life.

It is imperative that we get these first four commandments fulfilled to ensure our entry into His Kingdom. Flesh and blood cannot inherit the Kingdom of God. This means eternal life is only for one born from above and born of the Spirit. Only they have this privilege and honor. Let's consider each of the four steps more deeply.

Repentance

Repentance means turning from your sin. The first thing that Jesus preached was repentance. Matthew 4:17 says: "From that time Jesus began to preach and to say, 'Repent, for the Kingdom of Heaven is at hand.'"

Mark 1:15b: "The time is fulfilled, and the Kingdom of God is at hand. Repent, and believe in the gospel."

Paul echoed this in Acts 17:30, "Truly, these times of ignorance God overlooked, but now commands all men everywhere to repent." Then, in Acts 26:19-20, he said,

> 19 Therefore, King Agrippa, I was not disobedient to the
> heavenly vision, 20 but declared first to those in Damascus and
> in Jerusalem, and throughout all the region of Judea, and then
> to the Gentiles, that they should repent, turn to God, and do
> works befitting repentance." (Acts 26:19-20 NKJV)

2 Corinthians 7:10 (NKJV) says:

"For godly sorrow produces repentance leading to salvation, not to be
regretted; but the sorrow of the world produces death."

Peter preached repentance as well. "Then Peter said to them, 'Repent
and let every one of you be baptized in the name of Jesus Christ for the
remission of sins; and you shall receive the gift of the Holy Spirit'".
(Acts 2:38 NKJV)

"The Lord is not slack concerning His promise, as some count
slackness, but is longsuffering toward us, not willing that any should
perish but that all should come to repentance." (2 Pt 3:9)

1 Peter 2:24 says:

"Who Himself bore our sins in His own body on the tree, that we,
having died to sins, might live for righteousness— by whose stripes you
were healed."

"We having died to sins might live for righteousness."

1 Peter 3:11-12 says:

> 11 "Let him turn away from evil and do good; Let him seek
> peace and pursue it. 12 For the eyes of the LORD are on the
> righteous, And His ears are open to their prayers; But the face
> of the LORD is against those who do evil."

But the face of the Lord is against those who do evil. Change your mind about the way you think. This brings a change in outlook and, therefore, a change in behavior; we begin to act differently. It is the true repentance preached by Jesus and the apostles.

Today, in our modern Western churches, this commandment directly from Christ is so rarely, if ever, preached. How do we miss the very first step of salvation? If he doesn't take the first step, how can a person take the second or third and continue to grow in Christ? Repentance must precede a confession of faith. Neither the Ephesians nor any other church we read about could skip repentance. Anybody can say a few convenient words, such as the sinner's prayer, if they believe it will benefit them. But if these words do not come from repentance or turning, they mean nothing and can be taken back within minutes.

Ask yourself how often you have witnessed someone do this—say a few words, and then act contrary to the words they have just uttered. It has to be repentance, and it has to be authentic. Too many people are introduced into the Church on a *confession of faith*. In other words, they "make a decision for Christ," "give their heart to the Lord," or "invite the Lord into their heart."

We do not read any of these anywhere in the Scriptures. These are not biblical ways to bring people into a relationship with God. God desires change in us because He wants us to come into His Kingdom and live the life He created us for in Him. But repentance is skipped, and people are expected to believe. How can one truly start to believe and obey if they have not repented and turned from their sin? How can we receive forgiveness without repentance? How can we obtain a forgiveness we are not asking for?

When we look at Jesus, we see His opening statements were "repent." The same is true of the messenger who came before to prepare the way of Christ the Messiah, John the Baptist: "Repent!"

Paul and Peter, in the same fashion, saw repentance as an absolute commandment from God to be insisted upon as part of conversion. Jesus continues this theme through the letters to the seven churches of Asia in Revelations 2 and 3 (these letters are of absolute importance as they are the only personal letters He ever wrote). His call to five of the seven churches was that they had to repent and turn from their sin. Jesus' call has never changed, and repentance is a daily call for all Christians.

Jesus loves us too much to leave any one of us where we were yesterday. A key aspect of life in Christ is becoming like Him. We are to continue daily to be conformed to the image we were created to manifest.

WHY, OH, WHY DO WE KEEP MOVING AWAY FROM HIS TEACHINGS?

Why do we want to embrace the false teaching continually? Scripture warns about what happens when His people follow false prophets. Look at how the Old Testament repeatedly spoke about false prophets and wolves in sheep's clothing. These men always told the people what the people wanted to hear and caused enormous damage and tragedy with their lies. The children of Israel were God's chosen people, but because they believed the lies, they were led to destruction.

The prophets who heard from God always spoke the Truth no matter what cost or rejection they faced because the people needed to listen to it. The Truth is the only source of life and change. The Truth is the only thing that can bring us back to God's Kingdom when we are wayward. When we are disobedient and prodigal, it is because we believe a lie, deceived by one who would destroy us. What other remedy is there for lies but the Truth? The Truth sets us free indeed but requires that we respond in repentance.

A Daily Activity

Repentance is ongoing; it never stops. Repentance is practiced daily. "Be ye perfect for I Am perfect." (Mt 5:48)

When you kneel before Him, ask Jesus this question, "Is there anything in my life that offends you?" He will answer you because Jesus chastises those whom He loves so that He can develop and deepen His relationship with them. This is a marvelous way to start hearing from Jesus and to start a relationship with Him. It tells Him that you love the truth more than the lie, even when it causes temporary discomfort on the road to freedom.

How to Identify False Teaching

False teaching can be identified quickly. These teachings will always be about "I," "me," "my," "us," "we," or "our."

True teaching will always be about Him and how we can know, love, and serve Him. True teaching will bring conviction, greater love for God, easier forsaking of self, and greater peace within. False teaching will not lead to repentance, but true teaching will. True teaching brings about forgiveness because it brings repentance.

A sin not repented of is a sin that cannot be forgiven.

Belief

The second command of Jesus to obey to enter the Kingdom of God after repentance is to *believe*. To believe is to trust in Jesus, rely on Jesus, and obey Jesus. Each person's belief completely conditions our behavior; our entire life is driven by what we believe. In short, no matter what someone says they believe, you will know their beliefs by the way they live. You will know a tree by its fruit.

FAITH is BELIEF. In the Complete Jewish Bible (CJB), FAITH is the same word as TRUST. As we journey through this great adventure with CHRIST and as we mature and develop in HIS ways we will throughout trials develop a dependency on HIM. Occasions will continually arise that will create situations that will require us to either put our trust in man or place our complete 100% Trust in JESUS. These will be choices we will have to make.

From experience, I have been placed in situations where I had only one place to go, there was only one option, and that was to fully trust in the One Who can do it all. Through these trials of faith, my trust in Him grew exponentially, and my love and reliance on Him grew in the same magnitude.

"If you love Me, keep My commandments." (Jn 14:15) "He who does not love Me does not keep My words; and the word which you hear is not Mine but the Father's who sent Me." (Jn 14:24)

James tells us there is no point in just claiming to be a believer because even the demonic world knows and acknowledges that Christ is the Son of God. But demons do not trust in, rely on, and obey Jesus. "You believe that there is one God. You do well. Even the demons believe—and tremble!" (Ja 2:19 NKJV) To believe is to obey; you cannot have one without the other.

Believing is having a continued faith in Jesus. This continued faith builds our confidence and emboldens us to go further and deeper with Him to the point that there is nothing that we will not attempt—even raising the dead. This all flies in the face of the heretical theology of "once saved, always saved."

James also teaches us, "faith without works is dead." (Ja 2:26) He teaches us that our faith will be displayed to the world by the works that we do. Faith in Jesus manifests itself in works. Faith is not how we feel. Faith is what we do because of what He has done for us. The Bible tells us that Jesus constantly went around doing good. (Acts 10:38) This is what one who has faith does.

Every Christian needs to ask this question of themselves. WHAT HAVE I DONE AND WHAT AM I DOING FOR OTHER PEOPLE IN MY LIFE EXPECTING NOTHING IN RETURN? Not what you have done or are doing for your family because that is for your benefit. We all need to ask this question of ourselves because one day, this question will require an answer from none other than CHRIST Himself.

John 3:18 says: "He who believes in Him is not condemned; but he who does not believe is condemned already, because he has not believed in the name of the only begotten Son of God."

John 3:36 tells us: "He who believes in the Son has everlasting life; and he who does not believe the Son shall not see life, but the wrath of God abides on him."

Reading these Scriptures in John helps bring context and true meaning to our beloved John 3:16: "For God so loved the world that He gave His only begotten Son, that whoever believes in Him should not perish but have everlasting life."

Yes, God loved His creation, and His deepest desire is that none should perish. But He gave us free will plus hundreds of commandments of love to protect us from ourselves and each other, saying, "Choose life and not death." (Deut 30:19) This is because we choose to abuse that free will and the commandments that He has given us.

Consider one act of disobedience: "taking drugs." How many lives are lost, how many families are destroyed, and how many crimes are committed in just one day because of drugs? If all drugs were removed from Earth, how different would our world be?

Someone will return with, "What about the good drugs?" My response would firstly be, can you name one drug that has been discovered that has not been abused? Secondly, we would immediately have to rely on God, making us enter a relationship with Him. Isn't that what life is all about?

John 6:40 says: "And this is the will of Him Who sent Me, that everyone who sees the Son and believes in Him may have everlasting life; and I will raise him up at the last day."

John 14:12 tells us: "Most assuredly, I say to you, he who believes in Me, the works that I do he will do also; and greater works than these he will do, because I go to My Father."

I have been so privileged to have seen these more wondrous works in action. Only one factor was evident in these fantastic events: "total belief with reliance on Jesus Christ." I have witnessed countless miracles and been blessed to be used by God to cast out many demons, and all in the name above all names, Jesus!

If we relied on God, we would just pray and expect; we would have altogether to remove ourselves from the situation with childlike faith and let Christ do it all.

"And this is eternal life, that they may know You, the only true God, and Jesus Christ Whom You have sent." (Jn 17:3 NKJV)

The stronger your belief in Jesus, the better you will grow to know and fall more deeply in love with Him.

Baptism

The third requirement to enter the Kingdom of God is baptism. Baptism will be birthed out of repentance and belief in Jesus. The new convert, realizing their state of sin and the filth that they are burdened with from the world, will want to be washed on the inside and outside to feel clean before God by having their sins washed away. Only the blood of Jesus can accomplish this.

They will want to go through the death and burial of their old life and be raised into a new life of resurrection and hope in obedience to Christ, who commands us to baptize and be baptized. This act then reflects Christ's death, burial, and resurrection.

Jesus did not leave us with a bunch of suggestions to pick and choose from according to which ones suit us and our lifestyles. He gave us clear directions and commandments that must be obeyed. There is no such thing as situational salvation or situational obedience.

Romans 6:1-4 says:

> [1] What shall we say then? Shall we continue in sin that grace may abound? [2] Certainly not! How shall we who died to sin live any longer in it? [3] Or do you not know that as many of us as were baptized into Christ Jesus were baptized into His death? [4] Therefore we were buried with Him through baptism into death, that just as Christ was raised from the dead by the glory of the Father, even so we also should walk in newness of life.

Mark 16:16 says: "He who believes and is baptized will be saved, but he who does not believe will be condemned."

Acts 10:45-48 tells us:

> [45] And those of the circumcision who believed were astonished, as many as came with Peter, because the gift of the Holy Spirit had been poured out on the Gentiles also. [46] For they heard them speak with tongues and magnify God. Then Peter answered, [47] "Can anyone forbid water, that these should not be baptized who have received the Holy Spirit just as we have?" [48]

And he commanded them to be baptized in the name of the Lord.

Galatians 3:26-27 says: "For you are all sons of God through faith in Christ Jesus. For as many of you as were baptized into Christ have put on Christ."

1 Peter 3:18 says: "For Christ also suffered once for sins, the just for the unjust, that He might bring us to God, being put to death in the flesh but made alive by the Spirit."

And then, in verse 21, Peter says:

> [21] There is also an antitype which now saves us—baptism (not the removal of the filth of the flesh, but the answer of a good conscience toward God), through the resurrection of Jesus Christ.

Baptism now saves you because belief saves you, and belief is demonstrated by obedience. To be baptized is to obey Jesus' command.

The Holy Spirit

We have already been talking about the Holy Spirit, but the fourth thing we must do to enter the Kingdom of God is to receive the Holy Spirit. I will take some time on this subject because it is a contentious issue that immediately separates the humble from the proud (or sometimes just the ignorant).

Water baptism is the most opportune time to ask Christians to invite the Holy Spirit into their lives because they are an open vessel, surrendered to the will of the Father. This makes them open to receive Him. And we will all know when they have received Him because they will speak in a new language, the divine tongue given by Jesus as a seal on them that they are His betrothed.

As we have just read in John 4, we must do it all God's way and not ours; there are no second options. Religion has concocted so many dishonest and distorted distractions to lure us away from the Truth, and we need to address them for this fundamental foundation stone of entering the Kingdom of God to be laid in place.

One of the Scriptures that has been misapplied and led to many counterfeit theological teachings is John 20:22: "And when He had said this, He breathed on them, and said to them, 'Receive the Holy Spirit.'" Jesus here is giving His disciples a dress rehearsal of what will take place on the Day of Pentecost, the birth of the Church. The breath is symbolic of the wind/Holy Spirit.

This Scripture must be read with the following Scriptures for its appropriate context. John 14:17 says:

> "The Spirit of truth, whom the world cannot receive, because it neither sees Him nor knows Him; but you know Him, for He dwells with you and will be in you."

Here, Jesus highlights the difference between the Spirit being with them externally, such as when He sent out the twelve and the seventy to do mighty works in His Name, and when the Spirit comes and dwells within each person internally. He is describing completely different relationships.

John 16:7 says: "Nevertheless, I tell you the truth. It is to your advantage that I go away; for if I do not go away, the Helper will not come to you; but if I depart, I will send Him to you."

Jesus clearly tells His disciples that the Holy Spirit cannot come unless Jesus goes away, and then He repeats Himself, adding it will be "Only when I depart/leave this world."

We now live with such ludicrous, damaging teachings in our churches as that of "the second blessing," "two baptisms of the Holy Spirit," and the like. In effect, what is being taught is Jesus didn't know what He was talking about, or maybe He even told a little fib.

When the lie of the "two baptisms" is taught, it is also conveyed that the first time we receive the Holy Spirit, He has to apologize for coming into our bodies and leaving all His power somewhere else and has to come back a second time and remember to bring His power, His gifts, and fruit with Him. How ridiculous and gullible can people become?

We have discussed in previous chapters my favorite passage of Scripture, John Chapters 14 to 17. They are an account of the Lord's "last will and testament." Knowing all things on the night before the greatest sacrifice ever offered to God, Jesus was so delicate, so careful with every word that proceeded from His mouth. In these four chapters of Scripture, on close inspection, you will see that JESUS focused on three main points:

1. We must love one another.

2. If we love Him, we will obey His commandments; if we don't love Him, we will disobey His commandments.

3. He must go and the Holy Spirit will come into our bodies and take His place.

Jesus focused twice as much on the second subject as He did on the first and twice as much on the third as He did on the second. It is worth reading these chapters to discover this for yourselves.

Why did Jesus place such great emphasis on the Baptism of the Holy Spirit? Because He knew two things would happen: First, we would come along and change it all. Second, He knew that humans are incapable of fulfilling the first two without the third. We could never love one another and obey His commands if we have not received the Holy Spirit.

THE GIFT OF TONGUES

God had given us His Son, His Holy Spirit, and the evidence of the Spirit in us, His language. But instead of gratefully accepting this, we want to pull a Frank Sinatra act and "do it our way." James tells us in his epistle that we were born with a saltwater tongue; we never had to be taught to say no or to tell a lie. These all come naturally. But God has chosen to give us a pure and undefiled tongue in which to converse with Him, one that we cannot pollute, which will allow us in an instant to communicate with Him His way in any place and at any given time.

James 3:6, 8-11:

> [6] And the tongue is a fire, a world of iniquity. The tongue is so set among our members that it defiles the whole body and sets on fire the course of nature; and it is set on fire by Hell.
> [8] But no man can tame the tongue. It is an unruly evil, full of deadly poison. [9] With it we bless our God and Father, and with it we curse men, who have been made in the similitude of God. [10] Out of the same mouth proceed blessing and cursing. My brethren, these things ought not to be so. [11] Does a spring send forth fresh water and bitter from the same opening?

Acts 19:1-7:

> [1] And it happened, while Apollos was at Corinth, that Paul, having passed through the upper regions, came to Ephesus. And finding some disciples he said to them, [2] "Did you receive the Holy Spirit when you believed?" So they said to him, "We have not so much as heard whether there is a Holy Spirit." [3] And he said to them, "Into what then were you baptized?" So,

they said, "Into John's baptism." [4] Then Paul said, "John indeed baptized with a baptism of repentance, saying to the people that they should believe in Him Who would come after Him, that is, in Christ Jesus." [5] When they heard this, they were baptized in the name of the Lord Jesus. [6] And when Paul had laid hands on them, the Holy Spirit came upon them, and they spoke with tongues and prophesied. [7] Now, the men were about twelve in all."

Paul now asks a very valid question: "Did you receive the Holy Spirit when you believed?" What was the outcome of Paul's question? The Holy Spirit came upon them, and they spoke in new languages and prophesied.

God could not make His introduction into a relationship with Him any less simple and yet more pure and beautiful than by giving a new believer this amazing gift of His perfect prayer language. This allows that believer to go to the deepest, most intimate places with Him.

So many saints approach God with the wrong attitude when they approach Him by asking for the gift of a new language instead of asking Jesus for His Holy Spirit. This attitude is because they have been told and are convinced that they have already received the Holy Spirit when they believed or were baptized. But in all of Scripture, there is no account of either of these things happening. Every believer who believes that they have been baptized in and have received the Holy Spirit without speaking in a new language needs to ask themselves these three questions.

1. Was my experience of being baptized/immersed in the Holy Spirit audible and visible so that any onlooker could see that previously I did not have this gift, and now I do?

2. Can I identify my experience of receiving the Holy Spirit to anyone who should ask by using the Scriptures?

3. Did I ask God until I received the Spirit as Jesus taught in Luke 11? (Most Christians I discuss this subject with have never even asked for the Holy Spirit.)

Here, I also need to clarify some other fake doctrines because they are not in the Scriptures.

1. Laughing in the Spirit: This is not in Scripture and is certainly not the evidence of being born from above.

2. Tongues taught by another: speaking in a divine language that only Jesus can give "cannot be taught by any human being."

3. Evidence of yelling out one word: That is not evidence and also cannot be found in Scripture.

When receiving the Holy Spirit, God has one requirement: a complete surrender to Him. When we reach this state of submission, something within us opens and allows the Holy Spirit to come and dwell within. Having witnessed thousands of people receive the Holy Spirit, I can attest to this one common denominator that happens to each of them: When they reach that point of complete submission, they speak in a new language.

Jesus, in Acts 19 at Ephesus, chose Paul to set in stone the four foundational Cornerstones upon which Jesus, through His Holy Spirit, would build His Church. Paul methodically takes the believers through each step very carefully to enter the Kingdom of God by being genuinely born from above. He is meticulous, not missing any detail in this fundamental teaching.

Firstly, Paul checks to see if one has received the Holy Spirit. Those he inquired of had not even heard of the Holy Spirit. Their previous teacher, Apollos, had obviously not been baptized in the Holy Spirit.

He did not understand or know how to teach this because he had no experience on the subject.

Secondly, Paul asks an excellent question: "Into what then were you baptized?" The Ephesians were also wrong in this area as they had not known the Baptism of Jesus, but only the baptism of John, a "baptism of repentance."

Thirdly, Paul checked what Apollos had taught them about Jesus to ensure it was correct. This, too, was significantly lacking, or they would have been baptized into the name of Jesus.

Lastly, Paul could see that they feared God and understood repentance because the baptism of John was a baptism of repentance. He needed to know that all the foundations were laid for a right birth into the kingdom, that they were prepared for a long walk with their Maker, and that their deep relationship could be built in Christ.

People will always struggle in their walk with Jesus if these four foundations are not implemented. Receiving the Holy Spirit is never automatic, or else why would Paul have asked the question: "Have you received the Holy Spirit since you believed?"

We cannot put God in a box, though so many try. We see the plain truth of Scripture and are not comfortable with it, so we modify it—we modify what it says to be more palatable to the culture. Maybe you are embarrassed to speak in tongues. Perhaps you cannot accept that, though you have ministered in power (such as the 72 before Pentecost), you are not yet full of the Holy Spirit. Humble yourselves and ask Him for this greatest of blessings.

The Day of Pentecost — The Birth of the Church

In Acts Chapter 2, we learn of the birth of the Church. Here, Jesus uses the newly Spirit-baptized Peter, the apostles, and the brethren to lay these four essential foundation blocks and phases upon which He can build His Church with the exact obedience following the commandments of Jesus.

Peter adopts the same approach as Paul in Acts 19 to birth the modern Church into the blood covenant of Christ and then build His Church with His Holy Spirit. I believe it is beyond argument that Acts 2 was the birth of the New Church. Jesus, the Christ, filled His temples and believers with His Holy Spirit so that He could now dwell within temples not made with human hands.

Acts 2:1-4:

> [1] When the Day of Pentecost had fully come, they were all with one accord in one place. [2] And suddenly there came a sound from Heaven, as of a rushing mighty wind, and it filled the whole house where they were sitting. [3] Then there appeared to them divided tongues, as of fire, and one sat upon each of them. [4] And they were all filled with the Holy Spirit and began to speak with other tongues, as the Spirit gave them utterance.

Verses 5-6: This event did not happen in the upper room, but in the Court of the Gentiles.

> [5] And there were dwelling in Jerusalem Jews, devout men, from every nation under Heaven. [6] And when this sound occurred, the multitude came together, and were confused, because everyone heard them speak in his own language.

Verses 17-18:

> [17] And it shall come to pass in the last days, says God, That I will pour out of My Spirit on all flesh; Your sons and your daughters shall prophesy, Your young men shall see visions, Your old men shall dream dreams. [18] And on My menservants and on My maidservants, I will pour out My Spirit in those days; And they shall prophesy.

Repentance starts with these words from Peter.

Verses 22-24:

> [22] Men of Israel, hear these words: Jesus of Nazareth, a Man attested by God to you by miracles, wonders, and signs which God did through Him in your midst, as you yourselves also know— [23] Him, being delivered by the determined purpose and foreknowledge of God, you have taken by lawless hands, have crucified, and put to death; [24] whom God raised up, having loosed the pains of death, because it was not possible that He should be held by it.

Peter then pushes on with belief in JESUS — Trust in - Rely on - Obey the promised Messiah, the Son of David, the Son of God.

Verses 25-32:

> [25] For David says concerning Him: "I foresaw the Lord always before my face, For He is at my right hand, that I may not be shaken. [26] Therefore my heart rejoiced, and my tongue was glad; Moreover, my flesh also will rest in hope. [27] For You will not leave my soul in Hades, Nor will You allow Your Holy One to see corruption. [28] You have made known to me the ways of life; You will make me full of joy in Your presence." [29] Men and brethren, let me speak freely to you of the patriarch David, that he is both dead and buried, and his tomb is with us to this day. [30] Therefore, being a prophet, and knowing that God had sworn with an oath to him that of the fruit of his body, according to the flesh, He would raise up the Christ to sit on his throne, [31] he, foreseeing this, spoke concerning the resurrection of the Christ, that His soul was not left in Hades, nor did His flesh see corruption. [32] This Jesus God has raised up, of which we are all witnesses."

Verse 33 –The receiving of the Holy Spirit — the evidence is always seen and heard.

> [33] Therefore being exalted to the right hand of God and having received from the Father the promise of the Holy Spirit, He poured out this which you now see and hear.

The big question not only for them but for every believer follows:

Verse 37:

> Now when they heard this, they were cut to the heart, and said to Peter and the rest of the apostles, "Men and brethren, what shall we do?"

Then Peter, like Paul, carefully spells out the exact steps required by GOD for anyone who chooses to enter HIS Kingdom.

Verses 38-39:

Steps 1 to 4 are all the first four phases covered.

> [38] Then Peter said to them, "Repent, and let every one of you be baptized in the name of Jesus Christ for the remission of sins; and you shall receive the gift of the Holy Spirit. [39] For the promise is to you and to your children, and to all who are afar off, as many as the Lord our God will call."

Then, we have the result of obedience in following these first four foundational commands.

Verse 41:

> Then those who gladly received His Word were baptized; and that day, about three thousand souls were added to them.

This is what He told them would happen.

John 7:38-39:

> [38] "He who believes in Me," as the Scripture has said, "Out of his heart will flow rivers of living water." [39] But this He spoke concerning the Spirit, whom those believing in Him would receive; <u>for the Holy Spirit was not yet given, because Jesus was not yet glorified.</u>

We are blessed to have the straightforward simplicity of the teaching of Jesus in Luke 11. One should read all of Luke 11. To see the emphasis placed on this teaching by Jesus is to ask and keep on asking, seek and keep on seeking, knock and keep on knocking until you receive the Holy Spirit.

The Lord's Prayer

Why does Jesus answer the disciples' question about how to pray in the manner He did? We will see why when we break Luke 11 into three parts:

Part One

First, Jesus teaches them how to pray in verses 2-4. Then, He tells a story about the impertinent and pesky neighbor who will not leave his neighbors alone until he gets what he wants in verses 5-8. Why this teaching, this story in the middle of what He endeavors to relate to His disciples? What is the Master teaching them? After He presents this parable, Jesus tells them what to pray for: "Pray for the Holy Spirit."

"Ask and keep on asking...knock and keep on knocking...seek and keep on seeking and don't stop until you receive the Holy Spirit." (Verses 9-13)

I love David Pawson's story about his thesis on Acts 2 when he attended Bible college. He conducted a study and wrote a paper concerning the Day of Pentecost. His writing showed just how little he knew about what happened on that day. In short, he believed nothing happened and got an A+ for his thesis.

Many years later, now that he knows precisely what happened and has received the Holy Spirit's baptism, Pawson says if he wrote a paper about his experience and what he knows now, his Bible college professor would fail him. How many Christians know more *about* the Holy Spirit than *know* Him? What is more important? Is it to know Him or to know about Him? Is it to be in relationship with Him or to read about Him?

We can learn all the writings about Him, but how much more should we give Him a home within our being so that He can be our Teacher and Spiritual Guide 24/7, as we have constant communion with the Father, Son, and Himself, God the Spirit? Nothing man can teach even comes close to His teachings and His revelation.

If we are not baptized in the Holy Spirit and full of Him, how can we have His gifts and His fruit? How many people have come into the Church and are now functioning within the local church without this foundation in their lives that will allow them to be built on the Rock?

The Truth

The infilling of the Holy Spirit is one of, if not the most controversial topics among Christians. If it is not the truth, then why is it so controversial? We will swallow so many false teachings without question, but why not "swallow" this teaching? It is not difficult to understand why: to receive Him, a person must humble themselves, totally let go of self and surrender unto Jesus and His will. We have been conditioned to believe it is all about me and my control and recognition from man. People are unwilling to let go of self and surrender, so they will not go all the way with Jesus.

I have encountered several examples of people admitting they have not reached that place of submission to allow the Holy Spirit to come in. The vast majority instead choose to grievously rebel against the teaching of Scripture with, "You can't tell me I haven't got the Holy Spirit!" I am convinced that if the Holy Spirit can't convince a believer what they must do, I have no chance of convincing them. I have to leave that with them.

Two Examples

There are two outstanding examples of great men of God who waited many years for the baptism of the Holy Spirit. One is David Pawson, who I mentioned above and was arguably the most outstanding Bible teacher on planet Earth. Pawson took seventeen years from his initial place of repentance and handing his life over to Christ until his baptism. Throughout those seventeen years, he ran churches, preached, and taught his way around the world. On his admission, in hindsight, Pawson had the Holy Spirit with him, but when he was baptized, the Holy Spirit came into residence *within*. Then it was a very different experience.

What a man of God! When I was with David at the feast of tabernacles in Jerusalem, we were having lunch and discussed these teachings. He immediately put his right hand up to Heaven and said, "Lord, forgive me if I have ever taught this wrongly." In that moment, I witnessed humility at its pinnacle.

The second example of one who learned this lesson later is Smith Wigglesworth, who many will know about because of the remarkable ministry of works and miracles God called him into. Wigglesworth had 20 years of a preaching and healing ministry before he received the Holy Spirit. He is another example of the Holy Spirit *with* a man on the outside. This concept should not be hard to understand. In the Old Testament, this was the norm. When David and his mighty men were "covered" in the Spirit for mighty miracles of battle, it was not an infilling. When Saul was "filled with the Spirit" to prophesy, it was not like Pentecost. Even when Elizabeth, the cousin of the mother of our Lord, heard Mary's approach, her baby, who would one day baptize the Savior of the World, was "filled with the Spirit" in the Old Testament way. The Spirit was with John the Baptizer, but not indwelling. No, what happened at Pentecost was new, but for one example: the baptism of Christ.

> [13] Then Jesus came from Galilee to John at the Jordan to be baptized by him. [14] And John *tried to* prevent Him, saying, "I need to be baptized by You, and are You coming to me?"

> [15] But Jesus answered and said to him, "Permit *it to be so* now, for thus it is fitting for us to fulfill all righteousness." Then he allowed Him.

> [16] When He had been baptized, Jesus came up immediately from the water; and behold, the heavens were opened to Him, and He saw the Spirit of God descending like a dove and alighting upon Him. [17] And suddenly a voice *came* from Heaven, saying, "This is My beloved Son, in Whom I am well pleased." (Mt 3:13-17)

Try to understand how close God wants to be with us. Can one get any closer than being inside of a human being dwelling within them? How much preaching about the Holy Spirit is done weekly in churches worldwide by men who have never been introduced to or filled with the Holy Spirit? We all have to be careful that we don't fall into the same trap that Israelites fell into when they resisted the Holy Spirit as we read about in Acts 7 verse 51 when Stephen was martyred: "You always resist the Holy Spirit as your fathers did."

The miracles only come through the Holy Spirit. Jesus, Himself, did not do one miracle or preach one sermon until He received the Holy Spirit! Mark 16:15-18 tells us:

> [15] And He said to them, "Go into all the world and preach the gospel to every creature. [16] He who believes and is baptized will be saved, but he who does not believe will be condemned. [17] And these signs will follow those who believe: In My name, they will cast out demons; they will speak with new tongues; [18] they will take up serpents; and if they drink anything deadly, it will by no means hurt them; they will lay hands on the sick, and they will recover."

1 Corinthians 14:2 and 39: This chapter, when read in its complete context, is about how we operate the gifts of the Holy Spirit within a local church setting.

"For he who speaks in a tongue does not speak to men but to God, for no one understands him; however, in the Spirit, he speaks mysteries."

1 Corinthians 14:14: "For if I pray in a tongue, my spirit prays, but my understanding is unfruitful."

1 Corinthians 14:22: "Therefore, tongues are for a sign, not to those who believe but to unbelievers; but prophesying is not for unbelievers but for those who believe."

1 Corinthians 14:39: "Therefore, brethren, desire earnestly to prophesy, and do not forbid to speak with tongues."

I have asked many believers to please explain to me how a person prays in the Holy Spirit without speaking in a new language. Without exception, I have only received unscriptural and lame answers to this question.

Jude 1:20-21:

> [20] But you, beloved, building yourselves up on your most holy faith, praying in the Holy Spirit, [21] keep yourselves in the love of God, looking for the mercy of our Lord Jesus Christ unto eternal life.

We cannot preach a "McDonald's" style of entering the Kingdom of God. "Say the sinner's prayer. Make a decision for Christ. Invite Him into your heart." Jesus did not say to go into the world and get decisions. He clearly told us to go into the world and make disciples. Matthew 28:18-20 says:

> [18] And Jesus came and spoke to them, saying, "All authority has been given to Me in Heaven and on Earth. [19] Go therefore and make disciples of all the nations, baptizing them in the name of the Father and of the Son and of the Holy Spirit, [20] teaching them to observe all things that I have commanded you; and lo, I am with you always, *even* to the end of the age." Amen.

Make Disciples of all the nations.

Baptize them in the name of the Father, the Son, and the Holy Spirit.

Teach them to *obey My commandments.*

Jesus, in His proposal to us, His Bride, asks us these questions: Will you...

1 -Turn from all others to Me? REPENT.

2 - Choose only Me and continue to fall deeply in love with Me? FAITH.

3 - Be washed and purified? BAPTIZED.

4 - Be filled with the power and strength to obey My commandments, continuously displaying Your love for Me? "RECEIVE my Holy Spirit."

We cannot be Binitarian; we have to be Trinitarian. We need all Three Persons: the Father, the Son, and the Holy Spirit. 1 Corinthians 15:50 says: "Now this I say, brethren, that flesh and blood cannot inherit the Kingdom of God; nor does corruption inherit incorruption."

DISOBEDIENCE GOT MANKIND KICKED OUT OF GOD'S KINGDOM.

OBEDIENCE IS THE ONLY THING THAT WILL GET A MAN OR A WOMAN BACK INTO GOD'S KINGDOM.

IT IS HIS PLAN, HIS CREATION, HIS UNIVERSE, HIS WORLD/PLANET, HIS SON, HIS HOLY SPIRIT, HIS DIVINE NEW LANGUAGE.

***A "must-read" book is David Pawson's *The Normal Christian Birth*.

CHAPTER 7:
WALKING IN THE AUTHORITY OF
YESHUA HAMASHIACH
Where Does This Authority Come From?

I said in an earlier chapter that we never are to declare or bind in Jesus's name and that doing so would be arrogant and presumptuous. So then, how are we to walk in the authority of Jesus? Jesus gave authority over the twelve and then the seventy to heal the sick, cast out demons, and proclaim the Kingdom of God. How does He give authority to His Church today?

THE KEY IS BEING YOKED TOGETHER WITH JESUS TAKING THE LEAD, AND WE THEN SIMPLY GO ALONG FOR THE RIDE.

John 15:5 says: "For without Me you can do nothing." This authority has to come totally from Jesus. If He is not our Senior Partner, walking in His authority is impossible. He must be there with us.

To help bring this teaching into context, I want to share two of my personal experiences on the missionary frontline. The first story will illustrate what is required to walk in the authority of Christ. The second will show the opposite: how *not* to walk in His authority.

INDIA

On October 19th, 2019, I flew into Kolkata and then flew back to Australia on November 6th. In just under three weeks, we held gatherings in Raipur, Kolkata, Siliguri, Gangtok and Jehanabad. On average, 200-250 attendees were at each venue except for Jehanabad, where the Church had more than 450 brothers and sisters in Christ, and many onlookers attended.

In my 35-year walk with my Lord, I have never experienced such an intense time of ministry. There were healings, people filled with the Holy Spirit, and demons being cast out who were just told to "go, in Jesus' name" as the new King was coming in. It was a powerful time of great ministry and people being set free from the works of darkness.

The work started in Raipur, where 200-250 pastors and leaders were in attendance. It was a slower beginning to the trip, but over the three days, many attendees received the Baptism of the Holy Spirit (see Chapter 6). Many believers, if not all, went home with the infilling of the Holy Spirit.

Over years of missionary work, the Lord has graciously shown me how to engage with the people attending these workshops. He has also taught me how to teach as He would, as I have absolutely no skills as a teacher on my own. Here is how He has taught: He has me do a teaching session that generally lasts about an hour, and then at the end of each session, we open the floor for questions. This gets the people involved and stops them from walking away with doubts about their unanswered questions.

It has also taught me how to rely on Him and trust Him. If He does not supply the answers, I will be left exposed like a sitting duck ready for the hunter's bullet! Walking in His authority is impossible if we are self-reliant.

But in all these teachings, I have been privileged to conduct over the years, I have not had it happen once; He has never left me without His answer. I am reminded of Jesus' promise to His disciples. He said that if they were ever dragged before the courts and questioned, they should not prepare their remarks in advance because His Holy Spirit would tell them what to say. I have not been dragged before the courts, but the Holy Spirit has never failed me in any situation in which I was expected to communicate powerful truths of the Kingdom of God.

Back to the India trip. Next, we did a very similar workshop in Kolkata, which achieved results similar to the other ones. From there, we flew up to Siliguri, and I must admit that I was astounded at what happened. It was nothing short of miraculous to be involved in such a staggering and undeniable move of God and used by the hand of God.

I entered the workshop expecting it to be very similar to the previous two workshops, but it intensified over the two days as God, the Holy Spirit, made His presence so thickly manifest and moved so powerfully in the people. The following is just one story of what took place. Over the two full days, we did four sessions daily, and at the end of each session, I would open to the congregations to come to the stage to invite the Holy Spirit to come and abide within each of them. God wanted to make His home in their earthen vessels.

Throughout the teachings, after every session, I observed a young Indian lady who would have been between 25 and 30 years old. She looked troubled as she walked from one open window to another, just staring out, perplexed and struggling deeply within herself. That she struggled showed in her manner and on her face.

This young lady was very distinctive as she was dressed from head to toe in white and even had a headdress of white that left only her face open. She could have been easily mistaken for a Muslim. On each of the occasions when the people came to the front and invited the Holy Spirit to come and abide within, this young girl would faithfully come down to be prayed for to receive the Holy Spirit and begin to speak in tongues, as is attested in the Book of Acts (see Chapter 6). At this point, she did not receive the Holy Spirit.

At the end of the two days, all the meetings were being wound up by a faithful man of God whose name is Arjun. He is the lead pastor for that particular region in the northeast of India for the New India Church of God. (NICOG)

Arjun is a loving and open brother who embraces everyone one with empathy and compassion and who lives his life opening his home and church to whosoever may come. As Arjun was making his closing statement to wrap up the workshops, I could just catch (because of the language barrier) what he was saying about a recent event that had taken place in one of the dorms at his residence. He was telling us all that when he entered one of these buildings, he saw someone levitating above her bed.

I was sitting next to Binu, the overall leader of the North India group, and I turned and nudged him and said, "That can't be right." I thought I misheard Arjun saying, "Someone levitating," but Arjun is not one to exaggerate on any subject, particularly something like this.

Binu then explained to me that this is not an uncommon occurrence in India. He then explained a situation that happened to him and his siblings when he was younger. He and his brother, Biju, and their two sisters were in their hometown of Kerala, and on the streets, they saw a man levitating people off the ground in public. They said to each other, "Let's start praying in tongues and see what happens." When they did, the levitating immediately stopped, and the man carrying out these demonic happenings went ballistic, yelling and screaming. So, they ran, not knowing what to do next. I accepted the explanation, and then we prayed for the people's needs—healings, provision, and other things as they asked.

As we were about to leave the venue, Arjun and two of the other pastors with him approached me to come and pray for the young lady dressed in white whom they had proceeded to bring over and sit in front of me. When I knelt to pray for her, the young woman moved back and started to vigorously tap the side of her face with her hand and fingers at her temple. She was obviously in great torment as she talked and pleaded with Arjun. I asked Arjun what was happening, and he explained to me that she had voices going on inside of her head.

I immediately knew she was possessed by one, if not more than one, demon, so I proceeded to get back on my knees and pray in Jesus' name that they depart from her, simply calling on the name and the power of that name, JESUS, no frills, no added theater or drama, just His name, just Him and Him alone.

It took about 15 to 20 minutes of prayer, and then suddenly, this beautiful, rich language poured out of the young woman's mouth. I was stunned and pushed myself back to see this glowing smile across her face with just a few tears running down her cheeks. She was released and filled with the Holy Spirit. I continued to pray with her for a short time just so that I could enjoy and share the presence of God with her.

I then stood up and chatted with Arjun about the plans for the coming days.

Binu immediately came in and sat next to the girl, shared with her the love of God, and assured her that she would be okay now that God was living within her. He told her that God would never leave her.

Binu and I then said our goodbyes as we were due to go to the airport to catch our next flight. As we were walking out of the meeting place, Binu turned to me and told me, "Do you know, Dan, that while you were praying for that young girl, she told me she had a vision and that she saw two angels come down and take something out of her body and fly away with it?" I was amazed. Then, to add even more glory to Jesus, I'll tell you the story does not end there. After we returned to our hotel and were on the way to the airport, I learned that Arjun had revealed to Binu that this same girl was the one he had spoken about, who he had found levitating! This alone would be an amazing story, but it goes even further!

We flew back to Kolkata, out to Patna, and then drove the next day to Jehanabad. I was there accompanied by another one of the pastors, Binu's right-hand man, Brother Abraham. On the drive from Patna to Jehanabad, Abraham was caught up in a mobile conversation that I can only say was lengthy, for it was well over one hour. Arjun had called him to let him know that all hell had broken loose. He said the young lady in white had escaped from the neighboring country of Bhutan. She was married to a very wealthy man who had gained his money by exploiting this young lady as a witch, medium, and sorceress. Now, he was so angry at being robbed of his livelihood that he went to the authorities to cause as much trouble as possible.

Things were in an uproar.

We can read a similar account in Acts 16, where Paul cast a demon out of a young lady in similar circumstances, the same commotion erupted. Jesus is the same today, yesterday, and forever!

So, what do you think might have happened? We have a great, big, and wonderful God, and here is the most wonderful part: I have since received videos from the young woman and her husband, both thanking me for what Jesus did in their lives.

The icing on all this is that this young couple, husband and wife, now live with Arjun and his team in Nagrakata, northeast India, and the husband is now Arjun's number one evangelist, bringing many souls into the Kingdom of God!

My last communication with Arjun concerning what is now happening in his region (which was only last week) was more than encouraging. I will repeat him in his words: "It is like a river!" He kept repeating this as to what God is doing there among the Indian people. What a Savior we have and share!

How Not to Cast out a Demon

After all this, I was on another missionary trip. I tell this story to my shame (thankfully, God forgives!). I was in Hyderabad attending a church meeting. The meeting had finished, and we were all in prayer for the Church's needs when a young woman, maybe in her late teens or early twenties, began screaming at the top of her lungs with an almost deafening shrill.

I decided to go over and cast the demon out. I had seen and done this in many other occurrences, and this was a clear sign of demon possession. I said to myself, "Shall we cast this demon out?" What a mistake; what pride? Particularly when I know that it is only Jesus Who can, with no human intervention, cast a demon out of a person. I made the same mistake as the sons of Sceva in Acts 19:13-16 who took it upon themselves to cast a demon out, with no authority of Christ. Furthermore, they had no Holy Spirit.

> [13] Then some of the itinerant Jewish exorcists took it upon themselves to call the name of the Lord Jesus over those who had evil spirits, saying, "We exorcize you by the Jesus Whom Paul preaches." [14] Also, there were seven sons of Sceva, a Jewish chief priest, who did so. [15] And the evil spirit answered and said, "Jesus I know, and Paul I know; but who are you?" [16]

> Then the man, in whom the evil spirit was, leaped on them, overpowered them, and prevailed against them so that they fled out of that house naked and wounded. (NKJV)

That ended badly for them; the same could have happened to me.

This young lady was manifesting in a way I had not seen before; when she was screaming, her tongue came out of her mouth like a lizard's. I had never witnessed anything like it, and as hard as I tried, I could not cast this demon out of her, which is one of my greatest regrets today.

Later, I was told her story. Six months before this her entire family of six was traveling in a car, and she alone was traveling in another car. The first car crashed, and everyone in it was killed, leaving her completely alone. This poor young woman, in a state of overwhelming loss and confusion, went searching for an answer to her anguish, went to the wrong places, and opened herself up to the demonic world, a world that is happy to comply when asked.

When I tried to cast out this demon, I forgot I could do nothing. I commanded, I cajoled, and I even begged these demons to go, but it was only later, when it was too late, that God revealed to me my error. How could I have forgotten that nothing in me can accomplish this apart from the Holy Spirit of Jesus? Why did I tell Him, "I've got this?" Why didn't I say, "Lord, she is yours. What would you have me do?"

I have endeavored to find that young girl again and pray that Jesus sends her someone more sensitive than I was; my heart and I know that the heart of Jesus grieves for her. This is one of the many unfortunate situations where the enemy preys on the innocent and the hurting in this way, and if I'd remembered Whose job it was to rescue her, things would have gone differently.

I don't want to finish this chapter with a focus on the enemy. He doesn't deserve it. I would like to tell you about another missionary trip where Jesus moved powerfully, as this has been the norm, especially when I am surrendered to Him and His agenda. In Jehanabad, we were ministering in a fellowship numbering between 400 and 500 people. Because of the size of the room, they were literally spilling out of the building, and one had to walk sideways to get to the front of the Church.

When I arrived, I got out of the car to take my first step into the small building through a side door where all the believers and non-believers were crammed. About twenty meters away, down near the stage, two demon-possessed young women manifested. When I say someone "manifested," what I mean is that the demons inside made their presence known by affecting the behavior of the oppressed or possessed individual. These behaviors would often occur when Jesus entered a room with oppressed people. It seemed His presence brought pain and anguish, making them want to escape.

They went berserk, screaming and yelling, throwing themselves up and down, and shaking their bodies in a frenzy. I looked over to see them, and Jesus stepped in and took control. He walked me over to the young ladies and cast out the two demons.

As soon as I reached out my hand and placed it on the forehead of the first of the young girls, her eyes completely rolled back in her head, exposing what could only be described as two balls of puss in her eye sockets. When I prayed with both of them, one after the other (try praying for a person with another person manifesting right next to you; it's interesting), each one of them through "the authority of Jesus" — just invoking His name, His authority, each one simply melted down onto the floor, set free from the demons, and were able to enjoy the fellowship and all that went with it from then on. Amazing!

We cannot be like the sons of Sceva in Acts 19. We cannot approach spiritual warfare, even as I have done several times, in my own strength. To be used by God to deliver those oppressed by demons,

You must be filled with HIS RIGHTEOUSNESS — not your own.
You must be filled with HIS HOLINESS — not your own.
You must be filled with HIS AUTHORITY— not your own.
Most importantly, you must be filled with HIS HOLY SPIRIT.

You will come unstuck if you are not, and it can be dangerous territory, so don't go there. At best, you will be unsuccessful. At worst, you will be hurt, physically and spiritually.

When one walks in this authority, a presence goes before that person. But I must stress that this only comes from the deep intimacy one experiences when spending time with Jesus; it has to be all Him. It is not 50/50 between Him and us. It is 100% Jesus as we surrender and yield to Him.

I also believe we can lose this authority when we move in any direction outside of His will. If you cannot remove yourself from those situations you will encounter of being outside His will and remove all distractions, then don't attempt to do what this requires the authority of Jesus to do. To "believe in" is to:

"Trust in" Jesus.

"Rely on" Jesus.

"Obey" Jesus.

I believe our Western churches are full of people who have opened themselves up to the demonic through pride, lust, and greed, and carry a demon within themselves. Even many of the Church leaders are home to demonic activity; these demonic beings do not need to manifest themselves as they are very comfortable in the hypocrite's body, with the outside looking all shiny and supposedly spiritually manicured.

I further believe that these occurrences will increase exponentially because we have recently witnessed one more Bible prophecy fulfilled, showing me the end is nearing. Read Revelation 12 to help understand the last days' prophecies being fulfilled. This chapter also goes much deeper into what is also to come.

The Need to Recruit More Warriors

These demons have no fear of being exposed because we don't have enough saints walking in the authority of Christ and are not filled with His Holy Spirit. 2 Corinthians 11:13-15 says:

> [13] For such *are* false apostles, deceitful workers, transforming themselves into apostles of Christ. [14] And no wonder! For Satan Himself transforms Himself into an angel of light. [15] Therefore, *it is* no great thing if his ministers also transform themselves into ministers of righteousness, whose end will be according to their works. (NKJV)

Paul does not hold back here, and neither should we. In the previous verses, Paul tells us how to identify these men and women. He tells us they will preach another gospel. They will not follow the teachings and Words of Jesus. They will teach the doctrines of men, such as the secret rapture and untrue cheap grace, and they will speak against the Holy Spirit and His signs and gifts. They will want to elevate themselves and not lift Jesus to His rightful place. They will be greedy, not sparing the flock, taking money from people who can least afford it. These signs that follow any church leader are their fruit and display the inner man or woman.

2 Corinthians 11:3-4 says:

> [3] But I fear, lest somehow, as the serpent deceived Eve by his craftiness, so your minds may be corrupted from the simplicity that is in Christ. [4] For if he who comes preaches another Jesus

CHRISTIANITY IS NOT A RELIGION. IT IS RELATIONSHIP

whom we have not preached, or *if* you receive a different spirit which you have not received, or a different gospel which you have not accepted—you may well put up with it!

Just think about this question: What was Judas' job when he was with the Lord for three and a half years? He was the treasurer for the group of disciples! And what was he doing all that time with the funds entrusted to him to look after? He was misappropriating them. These funds were being given to serve the ministry of Jesus, but he had his hand in the bag, stealing for himself and the lifestyle he wanted to set up for himself. That is why he eventually sold Jesus out for 30 pieces of silver, which was the price of an enslaved person in those days.

How did Judas hide what he had stolen? He couldn't buy new clothes or eat better food with it; that would have been too obvious. He would have been tucking it away, setting himself up. Today, what we see are televangelists/false apostles. They don't even hide it. They flaunt it with their mansions, jets, and massive temples–monuments to themselves. They seek adoration and positions of importance in the world and fame with all that (other people's) money can buy.

The Times

The times we now live in are identical to the days preceding the first coming of the Lord Jesus. Only John the Baptist declared the Word of God in those days because Jesus was coming to one nation, Israel. The second coming of Jesus is being preceded by many such men and women declaring the Truth to our broken world because He is not coming back to just one nation but to rule and reign over *every* nation.

Spirit-Filled

A saint must be immersed in, filled with, and overflowing in the Holy Spirit, Who enables them to walk in the authority of Christ. From experience, you will see that God, the Holy Spirit, goes before you,

210

convicting people of their sins. The demons manifest simply in the presence of the saint described above. Why? For the same reason, they shrieked in painful manifestation in the New Testament: the presence of Christ. And then Jesus moves in and proceeds to cast the demon out, heal the sick, and raise the dead.

I have previously covered the chapters of John 14 to 17 in how to be born from above to enter the Kingdom of God. Here, I have cited them to highlight what Jesus wanted to highlight. You can read about His desperation to get into the heads of His closest companions and the three major commandments that will enable His authority to be with them. This authority will exist no matter the trials and difficulties they will encounter.

The three commandments are:

Love one another. Surprisingly, this was the least important in that it carried the least number of Scripture references.

Obey His commandments. This was second in importance and was supported by the second number of Scripture references.

Receive the Holy Spirit. This was most important because, without the Holy Spirit, one cannot do the other two or walk in His authority. The greatest number of Scripture references supports this.

John 14:16-18 says:

> [16] And I will pray the Father, and He will give you another Helper, that He may abide with you forever— [18] the Spirit of truth, Whom the world cannot receive, because it neither sees Him nor knows Him; but you know Him, for He dwells with you and will be in you. [19] I will not leave you orphans; I will come to you.

John 14:12 says: "Most assuredly, I say to you, he who believes in Me, the works that I do he will do also; and greater works than these he will do, because I go to My Father."

John 14:15-18 says:

> [15] "If you love Me, keep My commandments. [16] And I will pray the Father, and He will give you another Helper, that He may abide with you forever— [17] the Spirit of truth, Whom the world cannot receive, because it neither sees Him nor knows Him; but you know Him, for He dwells with you and will be in you. [18] I will not leave you orphans; I will come to you."

John 14:26: "But the Helper, the Holy Spirit, Whom the Father will send in My name, He will teach you all things, and bring to your remembrance all things that I said to you."

John 15:26: "But when the Helper comes, Whom I shall send to you from the Father, the Spirit of truth Who proceeds from the Father, He will testify of Me."

John 16:7-15 says:

> [7] Nevertheless I tell you the truth. It is to your advantage that I go away; for if I do not go away, the Helper will not come to you; but if I depart, I will send Him to you. [8] And when He has come, He will convict the world of sin, and of righteousness, and of judgment: [9] of sin, because they do not believe in Me; [10] of righteousness, because I go to My Father and you see Me no more; [11] of judgment, because the ruler of this world is judged. [12] I still have many things to say to you, but you cannot bear *them* now. [13] However, when He, the Spirit of truth, has come, He will guide you into all truth; for He will not speak on His own *authority*, but whatever He hears He will speak; and He will

tell you things to come. [14] He will glorify Me, for He will take of what is Mine and declare *it* to you. [15] All things that the Father has are Mine. Therefore, I said that He will take of Mine and declare *it* to you.

As we grow deeper and deeper in Christ through partnering with Him and taking His yoke upon ourselves, He will teach us to walk not after the flesh but after the Spirit. We will grow in confidence, opening and exercising one gift after another of the Holy Spirit, and learn how to live out the ninefold fruit of the Holy Spirit. It will make us bolder and bolder to take and use His authority (having read praying in partnership with Jesus). He will teach us how to control our flesh so we don't bring division between ourselves and the Father because we are trapped in sin. Sin separates an individual from God.

It has to be all Jesus. There can be none of "self" in it at all—self and all forms of selfishness create a blockage. Jesus will also teach us how to let go and trust and give control of our lives to Him. We must be completely reliant on Him with no other options, no other place of support. Then He, and He alone, gets all the acknowledgment and glory.

I have had several personal experiences of being put into a situation where all other man-made options are removed. Christ is, and has to be, the only option and answer available. He then shines in a life like never before. I have also witnessed this in so many saints who have applied this same law of God in their lives by having to be completely reliant on Jesus: no doctors, no hospitals, no medicines or pills, no one else could do anything for them; it all had to be Him.

When Jesus sent the disciples out to walk in His authority and do the works they had seen Him do, the only things they could go with were His Words, His name, and His miracles.

Matthew 10:1-4 tells us:

> [1] And when He had called His twelve disciples to *Him,* He gave them power *over* unclean spirits, to cast them out, and to heal all kinds of sickness and all kinds of disease. [2] Now the names of the twelve apostles are these: first, Simon, who is called Peter, and Andrew his brother; James the *son* of Zebedee, and John his brother; [3] Philip and Bartholomew; Thomas and Matthew the tax collector; James the *son* of Alphaeus, and Lebbaeus, whose surname was Thaddaeus; [4] Simon the Canaanite, and **Judas Iscariot, who also betrayed Him."**

Then, in verses 5-8, we see their obedience:

> [5] These twelve Jesus sent out and commanded them, saying: "Do not go into the way of the Gentiles, and do not enter a city of the Samaritans. [6] But go rather to the lost sheep of the house of Israel. [7] And as you go, preach, saying, 'The Kingdom of Heaven is at hand'. [8] Heal the sick, cleanse the lepers, raise the dead, cast out demons. Freely you have received, freely give."

Discipling is relatively simple. First, they watched Jesus do it, then they did it together, and then He said, "Now you go and do it."

Matthew 10:9-15 continues:

> [9] Provide neither gold nor silver nor copper in your money belts, [10] nor bag for *your* journey, nor two tunics, nor sandals, nor staffs; for a worker is worthy of his food. [11] Now whatever city or town you enter, inquire who in it is worthy, and stay there till you go out. [12] And when you go into a household, greet it. [13] If the household is worthy, let your peace come upon it. But if it is not worthy, let your peace return to you. [14] And whoever will not receive you nor hear your words, when you depart from that house or city, shake off the dust from your

feet. [15] Assuredly, I say to you, it will be more tolerable for the land of Sodom and Gomorrah in the day of judgment than for that city! (NKJV)

A Saint here has to be entirely out of their own control (no place here for control freaks) and completely reliant on their Lord and King. When I go to India, I must let go of my plans and my decisions. My entire trip is always in the hands of others; I don't know the itinerary, the places we will go, who I will meet up with, the accommodations—all of these I have absolutely no control over.

The same has been the case in the Philippines and PNG. In any of these countries and mission trips over the years that I have done, whenever I am in control, the authority of Christ cannot operate and does not function. It's difficult to explain and even more to understand. But, when you apply the principle, you see the results, as with so many other laws of God that we find so challenging to implement in our lives, e.g., giving, time management, and love (especially for enemies). In all these and many others, you must apply them in faith and then watch and wait to see how God works.

Trusting Jesus and Letting Go of Self

These principles are all based on trusting Jesus and letting go of self. The times I have gone all prepared with all my sermons down pat and with set agendas of precisely what God will do and accomplish, it isn't more than two days in that I have to put all my strategies in the bin and go with His. This does not mean one goes out unprepared. The preparation is in the weeks and months beforehand on your knees and in continual communication and relationship with Him. The preparation is spiritual.

These accounts in Matthew and Luke are very early in the ministry of Jesus, so the only thing the disciples had to place their faith in was what they had seen Jesus do and say. They would have declared, "We know this Man, and we believe that He has been sent from God, and therefore, we stand and declare in His name."

No one had even told Peter that Jesus was the Christ–the Messiah. In Matthew 16:16-17 it says:

> [16] Simon Peter answered and said, "You are the Christ, the Son of the living God." [17] Jesus answered and said to him, "Blessed are you, Simon Bar-Jonah, for flesh and blood has not revealed *this* to you, but My Father Who is in Heaven."

They had not witnessed Christ's death, burial, and resurrection, and of most importance is that they had not received the Baptism of the Holy Spirit, Who provides all the power to complete these fantastic works. What will be withheld from us, His saints, now that we have experienced all the above? I genuinely believe we will witness unimaginable things simply because Jesus told us we would do greater works. But one has to be on the front line making a stand for Truth in Christ as these greater works will not come from the back row.

If these men could do what they did with only the name and the Holy Spirit being *with* them rather than *in* them, what can we now not do?

Luke 10:1-2 says:

> [1] After these things the Lord appointed seventy others also and sent them two by two before His face into every city and place where He Himself was about to go. [2] Then He said to them, "The harvest truly *is* great, but the laborers *are* few; therefore, pray the Lord of the harvest to send out laborers into His harvest."

Luke 10:17-20 says:

> [17] Then the seventy returned with joy, saying, "Lord, even the demons are subject to us in Your name." [18] And He said to

them, "I saw Satan fall like lightning from Heaven. [19] Behold, I give you the authority to trample on serpents and scorpions, and over all the power of the enemy, and nothing shall by any means hurt you. [20] Nevertheless do not rejoice in this, that the spirits are subject to you, but rather rejoice because your names are written in Heaven." (NKJV)

Matthew 7:21-29:

[21] "Not everyone who says to Me, 'Lord, Lord,' shall enter the Kingdom of Heaven, *but he who does the will of My Father in Heaven.* [22] Many will say to Me in that day, 'Lord, Lord, have we not prophesied in Your name, cast out demons in Your name, and done many wonders in Your name?' [23] And then I will declare to them, 'I never knew you; depart from Me, you who practice lawlessness!'"

[24] "Therefore whoever hears these sayings of Mine, and does them, I will liken him to a wise man who built his house on the rock: [25] and the rain descended, the floods came, and the winds blew and beat on that house; and it did not fall, for it was founded on the rock."

[26] "But everyone who hears these sayings of Mine, and does not do them, will be like a foolish man who built his house on the sand: [27] and the rain descended, the floods came, and the winds blew and beat on that house; and it fell. And great was its fall."

[28] *And so it was, when Jesus had ended these sayings, that the people were astonished at His teaching,* [29] *for He taught them as one having authority, and not as the scribes.* (NKJV)

Jesus was under the authority of His Father. Scripture tells us here that we need to be under His *complete* authority by knowing Him intimately and obeying His commandments. *Then,* we can walk in His authority.

CHAPTER 8:

ETERNITY

What Will I Be as an Eternal Being with an Eternal Body?

Humans have contemplated eternity for eons. Perhaps you remember beginning to have these questions as a child.

> He has made everything beautiful in its time. Also, He has put eternity in their hearts, except that no one can find out the work that God does from beginning to end. (Ecc 3:11)

When we look into *eternity*, we must put aside all human thinking because eternity and the future are beyond all of us. Think of the great difficulty of trying to understand the here and now.

> [1] For we know that if our earthly house, *this* tent, is destroyed, we have a building from God, a house not made with hands, eternal in the heavens. [2] For in this we groan, earnestly desiring to be clothed with our habitation which is from Heaven, [3] if indeed, having been clothed, we shall not be found naked. [4] For

we who are in *this* tent groan, being burdened, not because we want to be unclothed, but further clothed, that mortality may be swallowed up by life. ⁵ Now He Who has prepared us for this very thing *is* God, Who also has given us the Spirit as a guarantee. ⁶ So *we are* always confident, knowing that while we are at home in the body, we are absent from the Lord.

⁸ We are confident, yes, well pleased rather to be absent from the body and to be present with the Lord. (II Corinthians 5:1-6, 8 NKJV)

Scripture is the only place we may find the answer. From Scripture, I believe that we, the people of God, will be taken through three stages of metamorphosis to reach our final eternal state of being One with the Father, Son, and Holy Spirit, no longer separated by the flesh and any of its impurities.

This is not something new. Just look around, and you will see so many examples of metamorphosis happening right before our eyes: caterpillars becoming butterflies, tadpoles becoming frogs, wrigglers becoming mosquitoes, and so on. Let's discuss the three stages:

Death to this World.
Life with Christ in the Millenium.
Life with the Father in the New Heavens and New Earth.

The first stage of this process that all human beings will go through is death to this world. We, saints and sinners alike, will become disembodied spirits that will return to the One Who made them, God.

The second stage will be reserved for the *saints alone* and will occur when Jesus returns to the Earth with all His saints who have passed from this life, plus all the living saints at that time to rule and reign with Him for 1,000 years in our new bodies.

The third stage of metamorphosis will happen at the end of the 1,000-year reign when God makes all things new: a new Heaven and a new Earth, including His new eternal children and bride. That state of being with God is the only acceptable intimacy that the Divine Holy God will be content with. God will be all in all.

THE TIMING

We have many writers in our Bibles who have written on this subject, but to clarify the second and third stages in this process, we will focus on John the Divine and the apostle Paul. Both men were privileged to have visions and revelations of Jesus that no other writer had, as far as we know. It is imperative to look at the timing of these revelations that were given to them. In seeing how they saw Jesus when they wrote these Scriptures, we will see how they perceived our future state of being.

The apostle John in his first epistle, Chapter 3:2-3 writes:

> [2] Beloved, now we are children of God; and it has not yet been revealed what we shall be, but we know that when He is revealed, we shall be like Him, for we shall see Him as He is. [3] And everyone who has this hope in Him purifies himself, just as He is pure.

When John wrote this epistle, he did not have the benefit of having gone through the Revelation of the ascended Christ seated at the right hand of the Father. I believe that what John is describing here will be our second stage of metamorphosis, that we will have a body like the risen Jesus.

Paul describes the revelations he had been given of the ascended Christ not only once but twice. The first time was at his conversion from being the worst enemy of the Church to becoming its greatest ally and evangelist. The second of Paul's revelations of the ascended Christ was when he was taken to the third heaven, as discussed in a previous chapter. These two revelations of Christ in His supreme state of being, allowed Paul to write with complete confidence the following words in Philippians 3:20-21:

> [20] For our citizenship is in Heaven, from which we also eagerly wait for the Savior, the Lord Jesus Christ, [21] Who will transform our lowly body that it may be conformed to His glorious body, according to the working by which He is able even to subdue all things to Himself.

Because Paul had twice seen the ascended Christ, he writes confidently about our eventual eternal state of being. Now compare that to John, who was hesitant in his writing, "It has not yet been revealed what we shall be," because he did not yet have the benefit of seeing our ascended Lord. Timing is everything.

Scholars' opinions vary on the chronological order of the writings of John. Still, one thing is not in doubt by anyone: the Gospel of John was written first (before his letters and Revelation), with most writers dating this between A.D. 80 and 89. Then John wrote his epistles (letters) between A.D. 90 to 95. Lastly, the Revelation was given to John around A.D. 95 to 98 when he was exiled on Patmos.

When John wrote the epistles, he did not have the advantage of seeing Jesus as He was revealed to him in Revelation 1. He had only seen Jesus as the One Whom he had lived with, loved, and walked and talked with for three and a half years, though he had also seen Jesus on the mountain at the transfiguration when He shone brighter than any earthly light.

John then saw the Risen Lord in His new body, which could disappear, reappear, and walk through walls, but when he wrote his epistles, he had not encountered Jesus as He is in Revelation 1. That is why he could only write about what he had already experienced when he penned, "and it has not yet been revealed what we shall be, but we know that when He is revealed, we shall be like Him, for we shall see Him as He is." (1 Jn 3:2)

Remember, this was John who was the closest that any person ever got to Christ when He walked on this Earth, and yet when he saw Him in Revelation 1, John fell face down as a man dead. He was so overwhelmed at the sight of this Amazing Being.

The chronological order of Paul's writings is also helpful in showing the order in which he saw the risen and ascended Christ.

First, Paul's conversion is dated 33 A.D. He was blinded at the sight of the risen Christ in this encounter in Acts 9. Second, we can read in 2 Corinthians 12, written around A.D. 55-56 from Macedonia, where Paul describes being caught up to the third heaven. So, when Paul describes his vision and says this vision was 14 years prior, that would date the vision around 41 A.D. Third, the epistles to the Philippians and Ephesians are dated 62 A.D. By then, Paul benefited from seeing Jesus as no one else had ever seen Him.

Second Stage of Metamorphosis

I believe that John, in his epistle, is describing the second stage of metamorphosis—the state of being that we will be throughout the millennium (1000 years) with Jesus.

Acts 1:9-11 tells us:

> [9] Now when He had spoken these things, while they watched, He was taken up, and a cloud received Him out of their sight. [10] And while they looked steadfastly toward Heaven as He went up, behold, two men stood by them in white apparel, [11] who also said, "Men of Galilee, why do you stand gazing up into Heaven? This *same* Jesus, Who was taken up from you into

Heaven, will so come in like manner as you saw Him go into Heaven."

These two angels are telling the apostles and brethren that Jesus will return in the same body as He left Earth; the reasons I say this are twofold:

First, if Jesus came back in His full glorified state of Being, as in Revelation 1, to rule and reign over this Earth for 1,000 years, could you even begin to imagine that Satan, having been loosed after being locked up for that 1,000 years could convince and gather the nations to rise and attack our Lord and His Saints. The Bible tells us this will happen at the end of those 1000 years.

Revelation 20:7-10:

"Now when the thousand years have expired, Satan will be released from his prison and will go out to deceive the nations which are in the four corners of the Earth, Gog and Magog, to gather them together to battle, whose number is as the sand of the sea. They went up on the breadth of the Earth and surrounded the camp of the saints and the beloved city. And fire came down from God out of Heaven and devoured them. The devil, who deceived them, was cast into the lake of fire and brimstone where the beast and the false prophet are. And they will be tormented day and night forever and ever."

Second, if at the resurrection of Jesus God had given Him this new glorified supreme body, and He walked this Earth in that state of Being, would there be one person on this planet who would have been able to deny that, not only is this Person the Son of God but that He is also God?

Whereas Paul was given his amazing insight into the Being of Jesus Christ, firstly at his conversion, and then at his being taken to the third heaven, he saw Jesus as no other New Testament writer ever had done until John later saw Him when he received the Revelation.

Paul's description of us becoming completely like Jesus will happen at the third stage of metamorphosis; this stage, seen by both John in the book of Revelation and Paul at his conversion and then again, his vision of the third heaven, saw what will be our final eternal state of being. What they both saw:

Revelation 1:10-17:

> [10] I was in the Spirit on the Lord's Day, and I heard behind me a loud voice, as of a trumpet, [11] saying, "I am the Alpha and the Omega, the First and the Last," and, "What you see, write in a book and send *it* to the seven churches which are in Asia: to Ephesus, to Smyrna, to Pergamos, to Thyatira, to Sardis, to Philadelphia, and to Laodicea."

> [12] Then I turned to see the voice that spoke with me. And having turned I saw seven golden lampstands, [13] and amid the seven lampstands *One* like the Son of Man, clothed with a garment down to the feet and girded about the chest with a golden band. [14] His head and hair *were* white like wool, as white as snow, and His eyes like a flame of fire; [15] His feet *were* like fine brass, as if refined in a furnace, and His voice as the sound of many waters; [16] He had in His right hand seven stars, out of His mouth went a sharp two-edged sword, and His countenance *was* like the sun shining in its strength. [17] And when I saw Him, I fell at His feet as dead. But He laid His right hand on me, saying to me, "Do not be afraid; I am the First and the Last." (NKJV)

Christ Himself has come to humankind in many different forms, and we are told about many of those. He was born of a woman and lived in human flesh for 33 years on this Earth. He was resurrected in a new body that was nothing like His previous earthly body; whenever He chose to reveal Himself in that new body, He could immediately be recognized as the Risen Lord.

Now, Jesus is unrecognizable as either of these two previous bodies when John saw Him in Revelation 1, but He still bears the scars of His crucifixion.

We know much about these three New Testament appearances of Jesus. Still, we are also privileged to have the Old Testament incarnations of Jesus when He revealed Himself on so many occasions and displayed the true image of God to humanity. He was the third man Who came to Abraham on their journey to destroy Sodom, Gomorrah, Admah, and Zeboiim.

Genesis 18:1-3:

> [1] Then the LORD appeared to him by the terebinth trees of Mamre, as he was sitting in the tent door in the heat of the day. [2] So he lifted his eyes and looked, and behold, three men were standing by him; and when he saw *them,* he ran from the tent door to meet them, and bowed himself to the ground, [3] and said, "My Lord, if I have now found favor in Your sight, do not pass on by Your servant." (NKJV)

Then, we read in the next chapter only two angels entered Sodom. Jesus let these angels go on to destroy these cities. Genesis 19:1 tells us: "Now the two angels came to Sodom in the evening, and Lot was sitting in the gate of Sodom. When Lot saw them, he rose to meet them, and he bowed himself with his face toward the ground."

He was the Rock that provided the water in the wilderness.

He was the fourth Man in the furnace with Shadrach, Meshach, and Abed-Nego.

He revealed Himself to Moses in the burning bush, and He was the One Who spoke with Moses face to face.

The list goes on and on. Jesus told us that God is the God of the living, not of the dead (Mark 12:27 Luk 20:38); He is the God of Abraham, Isaac, and Jacob—not *was* but still *is,* because they are all alive, and their spirits, as we read in Ecclesiastes, have been taken back to God. Let's look further into each of the three stages of metamorphosis.

STAGE ONE OF METAMORPHOSIS

Ecclesiastes 12:7 says: "Then the dust will return to the Earth as it was, And the spirit will return to God Who gave it." Solomon, the author of Ecclesiastes, was handicapped in his understanding of what is beyond the grave, as he lived in B.C. and not A.D. On the other hand, we are more than blessed to have a fuller revelation of all Scripture. Solomon did not have the benefit of Jesus' Words in the New Testament; he was limited in what he knew and could only express his understanding and could not see past the spirits returning to God; he could not see us having new bodies. Yet, incredibly, Job could attest that he would see God in his new body. Job 19:25-27 says:

> [25] For I know *that* my Redeemer lives, And He shall stand at last on the Earth; [26] And after my skin is destroyed, this *I know,* That in my flesh I shall see God, [27] Whom I shall see for myself, And my eyes shall behold, and not another. *How* my heart yearns within me!

John tells us the Words of Jesus. In John 5:25-29 it says:

> [25] Most assuredly, I say to you, the hour is coming, and now is, when the dead will hear the voice of the Son of God; and those who hear will live. [26] For as the Father has life in Himself, so He has granted the Son to have life in Himself, [27] and has given Him authority to execute judgment also, because He is the Son

of Man. [28] Do not marvel at this; for the hour is coming in which all who are in the graves will hear His voice [29] and come forth—those who have done good, to the resurrection of life, and those who have done evil, to the resurrection of condemnation. (NKJV)

1 Corinthians 15:42-44 says:

[42] So also *is* the resurrection of the dead. *The body* is sown in corruption, it is raised in incorruption. [43] It is sown in dishonor, it is raised in glory. It is sown in weakness, it is raised in power. [44] It is sown a natural body, it is raised a spiritual body. There is a natural body, and there is a spiritual body. (NKJV)

We can look at several descriptions throughout our Bibles and see what God can do with a "disembodied spirit." We can see how He can provide a body for them that can reappear and be seen. Matthew 17:1-3 says:

[1] Now, after six days, Jesus took Peter, James, and John, his brother, led them up on a high mountain by themselves; [2] and He was transfigured before them. His face shone like the sun, and His clothes became as white as the light. [3] And behold, Moses and Elijah appeared to them, talking with Him. (NKJV)

At the transfiguration on the mountain, who was with JESUS? It was Moses and Elijah.

We know and have read about the passing of these great men of God. Moses died and was buried by an Angel of God and the other, Elijah, never tasted death, but both men met with Jesus on the mountain before He had to face His exodus through His death on the cross.

Moses

> [5] So Moses the servant of the LORD died there in the land of
> Moab, according to the Word of the LORD. [6] And He buried
> him in a valley in the land of Moab, opposite Beth Peor; but no
> one knows his grave to this day.
> (Deuteronomy 34:5-6 NKJV)

God buried Moses.

Elijah

And it came to pass, when the LORD was about to take up Elijah into
Heaven by a whirlwind, that Elijah went with Elisha from Gilgal (II
Kings 2:1 NKJV)

Then it happened, as they continued on and talked, that suddenly a
chariot of fire *appeared* with horses of fire and separated the two of
them; and Elijah went up by a whirlwind into Heaven. (II Kings 2:11
NKJV)

Elijah was taken up to Heaven by a whirlwind, not in a chariot of fire.
Both men, who are alive with God, came back to this Earth and met
with Jesus on the mount of Transfiguration.

Then we have the account of King Saul, who had removed himself so
far from God that he sought counseling from a medium. Steeped so far
in witchcraft and demonic possession, she is known as the Witch of En
Dor.

> [11] Then the woman said, "Whom shall I bring up for you?" And
> he said, "Bring up Samuel for me." [12] When the woman saw
> Samuel, she cried out with a loud voice. And the woman spoke
> to Saul, saying, "Why have you deceived me? For you *are* Saul!"
> [13] And the King said to her, "Do not be afraid. What did you
> see?" And the woman said to Saul, "I saw a spirit ascending out

of the Earth." ¹⁴ So he said to her, "What *is* his form?" And she said, "An old man is coming up, and he *is* covered with a mantle." And Saul perceived that it *was* Samuel, and he stooped with *his* face to the ground and bowed down. ¹⁵ Now Samuel said to Saul, "Why have you disturbed me by bringing me up?" And Saul answered, "I am deeply distressed; for the Philistines make war against me, and God has departed from me and does not answer me anymore, neither by prophets nor by dreams. Therefore, I have called you, that you may reveal to me what I should do." ¹⁶ Then Samuel said: "So why do you ask me, seeing the LORD has departed from you and has become your enemy?"

²⁰ Immediately Saul fell full length on the ground and was dreadfully afraid because of the words of Samuel. And there was no strength in him, for he had eaten no food all day or all night. (I Samuel 28:11-16, 20 NKJV)

Another clear account that displays that God, in His Sovereignty, can re-embody any one of us at any time He chooses is when He did this with many bodies at the crucifixion and resurrection of Christ. The graves opened and gave up their dead.

⁵⁰ And Jesus cried out again with a loud voice and yielded up His Spirit. ⁵¹ Then, behold, the veil of the temple was torn in two from top to bottom; and the Earth quaked, and the rocks were split, ⁵² and the graves were opened; and many bodies of the saints who had fallen asleep were raised; ⁵³ and coming out of the graves after His resurrection, they went into the holy city and appeared to many. ⁵⁴ So when the Centurion and those with him, who were guarding Jesus, saw the earthquake and the things that had happened, they feared greatly, saying, "Truly this was the Son of God!" (Matthew 27:50-54 NKJV)

What did Jesus do for the three days and nights while His body lay in the tomb? Peter provides us with this answer in 1 Peter 3:18-20:

> [18] For Christ also suffered once for sins, the just for the unjust, that He might bring us to God, being put to death in the flesh but made alive by the Spirit, [19] by Whom also He went and preached to the spirits in prison, [20] who formerly were disobedient, when once the divine longsuffering waited in the days of Noah, while *the* ark was being prepared, in which a few, that is, eight souls, were saved through water. (NKJV)

Through these Scriptures, we can conclude that the spirits of man that return to God are all kept by God, waiting for the following two stages of transformation. We are not told much about where God keeps them in Sheol or Hades and how He keeps saints separate from sinners. We are not explicitly told either. Someone more knowledgeable than I may be capable of supplying us with the answer. Next, we will look at what is revealed about the second stage of metamorphosis.

STAGE TWO OF METAMORPHOSIS

1 John 3:2-3 tells us:

> [2] Beloved, now we are children of God; and it has not yet been revealed what we shall be, but we know that when He is revealed, we shall be like Him, for we shall see Him as He is. [3] And everyone who has this hope in Him purifies himself, just as He is pure.

If we read the books of Thessalonians and Revelation in context, Scripture tells us that this is what will happen. When Jesus comes back to this planet, as clearly depicted in Revelation 19, He will be coming with His armies of Heaven, complete with the saints, the martyrs, and those who have not accepted the mark of the beast or worshiped him or his image.

Upon His return, Jesus alone will strike at the world's armies, destroying them with the sword of His mouth (with a Word). One of these armies alone will consist of 200 million people, so how many millions He will slay, we don't actually know. This defeating and slaying of these armies have all been prophesied in Zechariah chapters 12 to 14.

Paul tells us that the dead in Christ on Earth will be raised up to meet this incoming army.
They will be joined by those who are alive in Christ, and they will all receive a new body and return to the Earth to rule and reign with Christ for 1,000 years.

1 Thessalonians 4:13-17 says:

> [13] But, I do not want you to be ignorant, brethren, concerning those who have fallen asleep, lest you sorrow as others who have no hope. [14] For if we believe that Jesus died and rose again, even so God will bring with Him those who sleep in Jesus. [15] For this we say to you by the Word of the Lord, that we who are alive *and* remain until the coming of the Lord will by no means precede those who are asleep. [16] For the Lord Himself will descend from Heaven with a shout, with the voice of an archangel, and with the trumpet of God. And the dead in Christ will rise first. [17] Then we who are alive *and* remain shall be caught up together with them in the clouds to meet the Lord in the air. And thus, we shall always be with the Lord. (NKJV)

2 Thessalonians 1:7-10 adds:

> [7] And to *give* you who are troubled rest with us when the Lord Jesus is revealed from Heaven with His mighty angels, [8] in flaming fire taking vengeance on those who do not know God, and on those who do not obey the gospel of our Lord Jesus Christ. [9] These shall be punished with everlasting destruction from the presence of the Lord and from the glory of His power, [10] when He comes, in that day, to be glorified in His saints and

to be admired among all those who believe, because our testimony among you was believed.

Add to that, Acts 1:9-11:

> [9] Now when He had spoken these things, while they watched, He was taken up, and a cloud received Him out of their sight. [10] And while they looked steadfastly toward Heaven as He went up, behold, two men stood by them in white apparel, [11] who also said, "Men of Galilee, why do you stand gazing up into Heaven? *This same Jesus, Who was taken up from you into Heaven, will so come in like manner as you saw Him go into Heaven.*" (NKJV)

Revelation 19:11, 14 tells us:

> [11] Now I saw Heaven opened, and behold, a white horse. And He Who sat on him was called faithful and true, and in righteousness, He judges and makes war.

> [14] And the armies in Heaven, clothed in fine linen, white and clean, followed Him on white horses.

Revelation 20:4-6:

> [4] And I saw thrones, and they sat on them, and judgment was committed to them. Then *I saw* the souls of those who had been beheaded for their witness to Jesus and for the Word of God, Who had not worshiped the beast or his image, and had not received *his* mark on their foreheads or on their hands. And they lived and reigned with Christ for a thousand years. [5] But the rest of the dead did not live again until the thousand years were finished. This *is* the first resurrection. [6] Blessed and holy *is* he who has part in the first resurrection. Over such the second death has no power, but they shall be priests of God and of Christ and shall reign with Him a thousand years. (NKJV)

1 Corinthians 15:44-45, 47-49:

> [44] It is sown a natural body, it is raised a spiritual body. There is a natural body, and there is a spiritual body. [45] And so it is written, "The first man Adam became a living being." The last Adam *became* a life-giving spirit.
>
> [47] The first man *was* of the Earth, *made* of dust; the second Man *is* the Lord from Heaven. [48] As *was* the *man* of dust, so also *are* those *who are made* of dust; and as *is* the heavenly *Man,* so also *are* those *who are* heavenly. [49] And as we have borne the image of the *man* of dust, we shall also bear the image of the heavenly *Man.* (NKJV)

In the second stage of metamorphosis, we will be given a new body in which our spirit will indwell. I believe it will be like the body of the risen Jesus when He walked and appeared on Earth for the 40 days after His resurrection, in which He appeared to many. This was the state in which, on one occasion, more than 500 people saw Him together.

I believe John was talking about this when he wrote his epistles because his understanding was limited to what he already saw and knew; John had not yet seen the ascended Jesus as He is now seated at the right hand of the Father in all His glory. The new revelation of Jesus, as He is shown in Revelation 1, came after the writings of his epistles.

What a glorious state of being that we will enjoy, clothed and equipped with bodies like the body of our risen Lord! How wonderful it will be to be with Him every day, not inhibited by this body of humiliation subject to many weaknesses and failings.

However, when we look at Scripture in its fullness, we can see that this will not be our final state of being; this will not be an adequate state of unity "as one" that the Father, Son, and Holy Spirit desire. He desires much more for us! Any separation, even this one in our new bodies, will not do for God's family with whom we will spend eternity with our precious betrothed Husband. From the laying of the first foundation Stone of GOD'S plan, His intention has always been that He should be "GOD, Who is 'all in all'". This brings us to the final stage.

THIRD STAGE OF METAMORPHOSIS

In Philippians 3:21, Paul tells us of God, "Who will transform our lowly body that it may be conformed to His glorious body, according to the working by which He is able even to subdue all things to Himself."

As I explained in Chapter 1 of this book, Paul was given the privilege of seeing Jesus Christ as He is to this day in all His fullness, firstly at his conversion in Acts 9 and then when God took him into the third heaven as he describes in 2 Corinthians 12.

Paul is saying here that in the new Heaven and the new Earth, our final state of being is that we will have a body conformed to the body of our Lord and Savior, as we read about in John's Revelation 1:12-17. Let us review this again to avoid any misconceptions about what this will look like.

Revelation 1:12-17 says:

> [12] Then I turned to see the voice that spoke with me. And having turned I saw seven golden lampstands, [13] and amid the seven lampstands *One* like the Son of Man, clothed with a garment down to the feet and girded about the chest with a golden band. [14] His head and hair *were* white like wool, as white as snow, and His eyes like a flame of fire; [15] His feet *were* like fine brass, as if refined in a furnace, and His voice as the sound of many waters; [16] He had in His right hand seven stars, out of His mouth went a sharp two-edged sword, and His countenance *was* like the sun shining in its strength. [17] And

when I saw Him, I fell at His feet as dead. But He laid His right hand on me, saying to me, "Do not be afraid; I am the first and the last." (NKJV)

What is this state of Being that we will be conformed to?

IS IT NOT PURE LIGHT - PURE ENERGY - PURE HOLY LOVE?

Put away all human thinking and ask God what He wants us to see. "What are You trying to show us?" I believe He wants us to be excited at the prospect of the closeness and intimacy that will come from being with Him in His glorious state.

When we consider God, Who is eternal light, love, beauty, righteous, holy, pure, noble, and then we reflect on ourselves in all honesty and how polar opposite we are with all our shortcomings and failings, then, and only then, can we see how we must go through these stages of change. How else can we be eternally living inseparably with God in our final eternal body? If any of us, even the very best of us, lived eternally as we are, can you imagine how much damage we would do to the new universe and all His new creation?

We live daily with the fact that God is pure, uncorrupted, unpolluted, undefiled light and energy, and we, humankind, are in darkness and seem to love to be in darkness. Because we love the darkness, this has caused us to live in a very dark world that is getting darker by the day. Humanity seems to be reaching for levels of unprecedented depravity and pushing ourselves to go lower and lower and further from God, Whom we are pushing out of everything to our detriment.

How do we now stop these deplorable atrocities and injustices that are played out on a global scale and brought to light through the production of movies like *Sound of Freedom?* There are untold numbers

of documentaries displaying the inequality, poverty, and sub-existence that so many people in our fallen world are forced to live under.
I can speak firsthand on these matters, as I have been there, lived in, and worked in many of the world's worst slums. I have worked with young men and women whose stories just make you want to stand there and weep for them and all the others who are suffering under this abuse. I once heard a young girl tell me she has "been made to feel like a human toilet." I just wanted to break, begging Jesus to return with justice.

Now, we are witnessing a new level of subhuman behavior of evil proportions after the woeful attack by Hamas on the innocent in Israel. We have country after country applauding these deplorable acts of indecency and screaming out for more of the same. There is not an animal on this planet that would stoop this low.

The Light

What are we saints doing when, even in our modern churches, we are chasing the darkness? We deliberately let in no natural God-given light and only want to produce manufactured light. What are we saying, and why would we not want to gather with the light of the World? Why do we prefer artificial, manufactured light? What do we want to hide or hide from?

We have become addicted to plastic in all its forms and love lots of "shiny things" that are all distractions drawing us away from the real pure light. These distractions lure us into one sin after another to the point that we have become hardened and calloused to sin, all the while knowing that all this manufactured sin pushes us further and further into darkness.

In the Words of Jesus within Chapter 3 of John's Gospel, the same chapter which contains the most quoted passage in the New Testament,

Christ tells us about man seeking the darkness rather than the light. John 3:19-21 says:

> [19] And this is the condemnation, that the light has come into the world, and men loved darkness rather than light, because their deeds were evil. [20] For everyone practicing evil hates the light and does not come to the light, lest his deeds should be exposed. [21] But he who does the truth comes to the light, that his deeds may be clearly seen, that they have been done in God." (NKJV)

As faithful Christians, our lives should be transparent so that all our deeds can be displayed and seen. What do we have to hide if our lives are holy and righteous? Ask yourselves this question: "What am I doing that I am ashamed of and having to do in the dark in my locked room away from the light?" With God, there is no place to hide or to hide anything you do.

The Godhead is pure light. Should we not strive to live in and display that light in our churches and every aspect of our lives? 1 Timothy 6:15-16 says:

> [15] which He will manifest in His own time, *He Who is* the blessed and only Potentate, the King of kings and Lord of lords, [16] Who alone has immortality, dwelling in unapproachable light, Whom no man has seen or can see, to Whom *be* honor and everlasting power. Amen. (NKJV)

1 John 1:5-7 adds:

> [5] This is the message which we have heard from Him and declare to you, that God is light and in Him is no darkness at all. [6] If we say that we have fellowship with Him, and walk in darkness, we lie and do not practice the truth. [7] But if we walk in the light as He is in the light, we have fellowship with one

another, and the blood of Jesus Christ His Son cleanses us from all sin. (NKJV)

John 1:4-5, 7-9:

> ⁴ In Him was life, and the life was the light of men. ⁵ And the light shines in the darkness, and the darkness did not comprehend it. ⁷ This man came for a witness, to bear witness of the light, that all through him might believe. ⁸ He was not that light but *was sent* to bear witness of that light. ⁹ That was the true light which gives light to every man coming into the world. (NKJV)

John 12:35-36:

> ³⁵ Then Jesus said to them, "A little while longer the light is with you. Walk while you have the light, lest darkness overtake you; he who walks in darkness does not know where he is going. ³⁶ *While you have the light, believe in the light, that you may become sons of light."* These things Jesus spoke, and departed, and was hidden from them. (NKJV)

Isaiah 9:1-2:

> ¹ Nevertheless the gloom *will* not *be* upon her who *is* distressed, as when at first He lightly esteemed the land of Zebulun and the land of Naphtali, And afterward more heavily oppressed *her, By* the way of the sea, beyond the Jordan, In Galilee of the Gentiles. ² The people who walked in darkness Have seen a great light; Those who dwelled in the land of the shadow of death, upon them a light has shined. (NKJV)

Revelation 21:22-24:

> ²² But I saw no temple in it, for the Lord God Almighty and the Lamb are its temple. ²³ The city had no need of the sun or of

the moon to shine in it, for the glory of God illuminated it. The Lamb *is* its light. [24] And the nations of those who are saved shall walk in its light, and the kings of the Earth bring their glory and honor into it. (NKJV)

Called to Be the Light

We have established that God is pure light that is beyond human comprehension. He is the source of all the light and life that exists in our universe and greater than any of these lights or stars because the Maker is greater and more powerful than what He has made. We Saints must be the light to set an example that would shine so bright and be so attractive that the people of this world are drawn to us like the sinners in Jesus' day were drawn to Him. They were drawn to the light because they could see more than this broken world offered, and their lives could be lifted higher, cleaner, pure, and holy.

Now more than ever, people will want something to hold onto as this world is shaken and in the process of falling apart all around them and in which every foundation that man has trusted in for centuries breaks down and collapses. There will be only one Immovable Stone, Christ, to hold onto.

It is refreshing and exciting to see the rebellion by commonsense people against this latest attack on God by those who are controlled by the enemy and by the society that behaves in a way that is disgusting to God. We are observing and will continue to observe this Scripture. "Moreover, the law entered that the offense might abound. But where sin abounded, grace abounded much more." (Ro 5:20) The worse man gets, the higher God will lift the bar. Through these great times of trouble, we will be exposed to one set of tragic events after another, each getting worse than the preceding one. Jesus calls these events birth pangs, and they must play out to their fullness to usher in the return of Christ. A "must-read" is Isaiah 24, like Matthew 24 on steroids!

Now, with our world that is so muddied and polluted with darkness and sin, we Christians grapple with what is true and pure selfless *agape* love. We would love to live out pure love; we would so much like to be the image that reflects Christ in this world's broken, fallen state, with this love as one great attribute of His flawless character, but we continually fall short. We simply fail because, as Paul tells us in 1 Corinthians 13, our vision of pure, selfless love is blurred, and we don't recognize what pure, selfless love looks like. This is why we continually fail to achieve this state of being.

1 Corinthians 13 is a resume of the character of Christ and His love, with these fifteen express summations of His Person. Slowly meditate on each of these attributes individually, and you will see for yourself that they speak of Jesus alone. It will show us how to mirror His character in our lives. Then, look at how opposite we actually are in our *own* characters.

The attributes are:

Love suffers long
and is kind;
love does not envy;
love does not parade itself,
is not puffed up;
does not behave rudely,
does not seek its own,
is not provoked,
thinks no evil;
does not rejoice in iniquity,
but rejoices in the truth;
bears all things,
believes all things,
hopes all things,
endures all things."

There has only been One Person Who has walked on this planet and totally lived out all fifteen attributes of love to their fullness. These are precise descriptions of Jesus Christ. 1 Corinthians 13:9-12 goes on to say:

> [9] For we know in part, and we prophesy in part. [10] But when that which is perfect has come, then that which is in part will be done away. [11] When I was a child, I spoke as a child, I understood as a child, I thought as a child; but when I became a man, I put away childish things. [12] For now we see in a mirror, dimly, but then face to face. Now I know in part, but then I shall know just as I also am known. (NKJV)

As previously pointed out in our final state of being we will no longer see true selfless love warped and distorted by this world, but we will be just like JESUS; pure, perfect love in all its complete fullness.

At the end of the age of this first creation, God will be all in all. What does this mean? What happens when GOD fills all in all? Because God is Light and Love, does that not mean that what He fills will become Light and Love, plus all the other beautiful and majestic attributes of God? 1 Corinthians 15:28 says: "Now when all things are made subject to Him, then the Son Himself will also be subject to Him Who put all things under Him, that God may be all in all."

Ephesians 1:20-23 says:

> [20] which He worked in Christ when He raised Him from the dead and seated *Him* at His right hand in the heavenly *places,* [21] far above all principality and power and might and dominion, and every name that is named, not only in this age but also in that which is to come. [22] And He put all *things* under His feet and gave Him *to be* head over all *things* to the Church, [23] which is His body, the fullness of Him Who fills all in all. (NKJV)

Colossians 3:11 says:

"Where there is neither Greek nor Jew, circumcised nor uncircumcised, barbarian, Scythian, slave nor free, but Christ is all and in all."

What Will We Be Like?

If all of this is true and we will have a body like the risen Lord, then we can reasonably conclude that because He is pure light, we will have a body that consists of and houses pure light. This concept simply leaves me overwhelmed.

When we meditate on what being with Jesus for eternity will be like, this life pales into insignificance with all its pain and futility. We will all have a new body just like His glorious body. He is light; we will be light, and we will also be pure energy; our bodies will function entirely on that light/energy. We would never again need to go to the toilet or eat food. We could travel at the speed of light. The list goes on and on past the greatest of any dreamer's dreams. A complete collection of Scriptures would need a book on its own, but here are a couple more that affirm what I am saying:

Daniel 12:1-3:

> [1] "At that time Michael shall stand up, The great prince who stands *watch* over the sons of your people; And there shall be a time of trouble, Such as never was since there was a nation, *Even* to that time. And at that time your people shall be delivered, Everyone who is found written in the book. [2] And many of those who sleep in the dust of the Earth shall awake, Some to everlasting life, Some to shame *and* everlasting contempt. [3] Those who are wise shall shine like the brightness of the firmament, And is those who turn many to righteousness like the stars forever and ever." (NKJV)

Remember that Jesus also told us this.

Revelation 21:22-23 tells us of the New Jerusalem.

> [22] But I saw no temple in it, for the Lord God Almighty and the Lamb are its temple. [23] The city had no need of the sun or of the moon to shine in it, for the glory of God illuminated it. The Lamb *is* its light. (NKJV)

Job 18:5-6:

> [5] "The light of the wicked indeed goes out, And the flame of his fire does not shine. [6] The light is dark in his tent, And his lamp beside him is put out." (NKJV)

Matthew 13:42-43:

> [42] and will cast them into the furnace of fire. There will be wailing and gnashing of teeth. [43] Then the righteous will shine forth as the sun in the Kingdom of their Father. He who has ears to hear, let him hear! (NKJV)

Even the angels are drenched in light. "I saw still another mighty angel coming down from Heaven, clothed with a cloud. And a rainbow was on his head, his face was like the sun, and his feet like pillars of fire." (Rev 10:1)

As I stated above, I believe that in the millennium, we won't have this final body because logic tells us that Satan is released at the end of the thousand years and gathers the world and its armies together to come and fight against our Lord and us His saints. If we had these final bodies, no one could ever imagine anyone attacking the Infinite One and His army.

At the end of this dispensation, I Father steps onto the scene and annihilates man one last time.

^{8} And will go out to deceive the nations which are in the four corners of the Earth, Gog and Magog, to gather them together to battle, whose number *is* as the sand of the sea. ^{9} They went up on the breadth of the Earth and surrounded the camp of the saints and the beloved city. And fire came down from God out of Heaven and devoured them. (Revelation 20:8-9 NKJV)

Can you imagine anything more closely knit together than pure light with pure light? This is the only eternal state acceptable to God, dwelling eternally with His children. As Jesus Christ Himself went through these phases of revealing Himself in bodily form, should we think it strange that He will take us through the same process? He will take us to the epitome of eternal human existence to be just like He is: pure light, pure love and pure energy.

CHAPTER 9:
THE FINISH
Why Did I Write This Book?

Look at the first-century Church and consider what had crept into their fellowship to be pushed upon the early Christians. We see this when we look at the letters Jesus wrote to the seven churches in Asia and how they were required to repent and turn from the corrupted messages they had allowed into their congregations through false teachers and false prophets. Five of the seven churches were commanded by our Lord to change their ways or suffer the consequences.

How many epistles were written to combat false teaching, false religion, false brethren, and false prophets? This all happened in an incredibly short space of time with men who walked and talked with Jesus, guarding the churches and the brethren. Could anyone measure what has now crept into our modern twenty-first-century Church over the last two thousand years, which is no longer under the stewardship of the early fathers?

This creeping is tragic but hardly surprising since Jesus and all the founding fathers warned us and described in detail this corruption and how it would come into the body of Christ.

Matthew 7:13-16, 21-24:

> [13] Enter by the narrow gate; for wide *is* the gate and broad *is* the way that leads to destruction, and there are many who go in by it. [14] Because narrow *is* the gate and difficult *is* the way which leads to life, and there are few who find it. [15] Beware of false prophets, who come to you in sheep's clothing, but inwardly they are ravenous wolves. [16] You will know them by their fruits. Do men gather grapes from thornbushes or figs from thistles?

> [21] Not everyone who says to Me, "Lord, Lord," shall enter the Kingdom of Heaven, but he who does the will of My Father in Heaven. [22] Many will say to Me in that day, "Lord, Lord, have we not prophesied in Your name, cast out demons in Your name, and done many wonders in Your name?" [23] And then I will declare to them, "I never knew you; depart from Me, you who practice lawlessness!" [24] Therefore whoever hears these sayings of Mine, and does them, I will liken him to a wise man who built his house on the rock. (NKJV)

These are all the Words of Jesus Christ, and they carry the gravest of warnings to all of us who believe: Don't mess with your walk, don't mess with His Words, don't mess with the Son of God.

Humans and times never change; we keep doing the same things repeatedly, expecting a different outcome. I think someone put it this way, "This is how we define stupidity."

In a 1948 speech to the British House of Commons, Winston Churchill said, "Those that fail to learn from history are doomed to repeat it." No matter the origin and occasion, the sentiments are eternal. Look at our world. We have learned nothing. When does man ever stop and seek God's opinion and guidance on what to do next? No, we just plunge headfirst into a rock pool of money, seeking the next buck without considering that this dive might break our necks.

Luke 6:26 says: "Woe to you when all men speak well of you, for so did their fathers to the false prophets." Jesus speaks to the religious leaders of His time and says things never change. I am resolute in saying that if He were here today, He would say the same things to modern-day church leaders.

If a saint carefully studies the Words of Jesus and meditates and prays into each one as they read each word, they will quickly discover that all false teachings and religion will be cast out of that saint's life. Jesus is the supreme schoolmaster. Let's let Him teach us.

Matthew 5:21-22, 27-28, 31-34, 38-39, 43-44:

> [21] You have heard that it was said to those of old, "You shall not murder, and whoever murders will be in danger of the judgment." [22] But I say to you that whoever is angry with his brother without a cause shall be in danger of the judgment. And whoever says to his brother, "Raca!" shall be in danger of the council. But whoever says, "You fool!" shall be in danger of hell fire.
>
> [27] You have heard that it was said to those of old, "You shall not commit adultery." [28] But I say to you that whoever looks at a woman to lust for her has already committed adultery with her in his heart.
>
> [31] Furthermore, it has been said, "Whoever divorces his wife, let him give her a certificate of divorce." [32] But I say to you that whoever divorces his wife for any reason except sexual immorality causes her to commit adultery; and whoever marries a woman who is divorced commits adultery.

[33] Again you have heard that it was said to those of old, "You shall not swear falsely, but shall perform your oaths to the Lord." [34] But I say to you, do not swear at all: neither by Heaven, for it is God's throne.

[38] You have heard that it was said, "An eye for an eye and a tooth for a tooth." [39] But I tell you not to resist an evil person. But whoever slaps you on your right cheek, turn the other to him also.

[43] You have heard that it was said, "You shall love your neighbor and hate your enemy." [44] But I say to you, love your enemies, bless those who curse you, do good to those who hate you, and pray for those who spitefully use you and persecute you. (NKJV)

In the Sermon on the Mount, Jesus tells His followers, "This is what you have been told; I now tell you the Truth because I Am the Truth."

He cut straight across every wrong teaching over hundreds of years, even concerning the Sabbath day, which He nailed down. Jesus made it so beautifully simple: "Is it good to do right or do wrong on the Sabbath day?" The scribes and Pharisees had taken one of the Ten Commandments and produced over six hundred to elevate themselves.

It is no different today. We just take His Words simply in their full application and they set us free from religion. Then, our reliance stands upon the relationship we have with Him. God has always intended His relationship with us to be One-on-one. There should not be a middleman between us and God. Think about it. How would you like a marriage where you had to go through a third party whenever you chose to communicate with your partner?

We are betrothed to Christ, and our only intermediary is the Holy Spirit, the Best Man, Who is preparing the bride for the marriage. Sadly, some people like to have a man in the middle because this limits their commitment. Someone once said those who heard God the most clearly and audibly were called to the most difficult mission. Most do not want a difficult mission and don't want to surrender completely to God's will. Keeping a man between themselves and God keeps it all nice and loose with God, and they can leave themselves in control.

But the opposite takes place. They are not in control because they become a slave to the lowest part of themselves in selfishness. Paul, Peter, and John have all warned us that we must be on the lookout to guard and protect our eternal spiritual lives.

Paul said in 2 Corinthians 11:13-15:

> [13] For such *are* false apostles, deceitful workers, transforming themselves into apostles of Christ. [14] And no wonder! For Satan Himself transforms Himself into an angel of light. [15] Therefore, *it is* no great thing if his ministers also transform themselves into ministers of righteousness, whose end will be according to their works. (NKJV)

In the same chapter, verse 26 speaks of the dangers of false brethren:

> [15] *In* journeys often, *in* perils of waters, *in* perils of robbers, *in* perils of *my own* countrymen, *in* perils of the Gentiles, *in* perils in the city, *in* perils in the wilderness, *in* perils in the sea, *in* perils among false brethren; (NKJV)

2 Timothy 3:1-5 says:

> [1] But know this, that in the last days perilous times will come: [2] For men will be lovers of themselves, lovers of money, boasters, proud, blasphemers, disobedient to parents, unthankful, unholy, [3] unloving, unforgiving, slanderers, without self-control, brutal, despisers of good, [4] traitors, headstrong, haughty, lovers of pleasure rather than lovers of God, [5] having a

form of godliness but denying its power. And from such people turn away! (NKJV)

Peter tells us in 2 Peter 2:1-3:

> [1] But there were also false prophets among the people, even as there will be false teachers among you, who will secretly bring in destructive heresies, even denying the Lord Who bought them *and* bring on themselves swift destruction. [2] And many will follow their destructive ways, because of whom the way of truth will be blasphemed. [3] By covetousness they will exploit you with deceptive words; for a long time their judgment has not been idle, and their destruction does not slumber.

And 1 John 4:1, 4-5 says:

> [1] Beloved, do not believe every spirit, but test the spirits, whether they are of God; because many false prophets have gone out into the world.
> [4] You are of God, little children, and have overcome them, because He Who is in you is greater than he who is in the world. [5] They are of the world. Therefore, they speak *as* of the world, and the world hears them. (NKJV)

These false teachers and prophets are forerunners of the False Prophet that is living and flourishing on our planet today, here and now working in alignment with their father, Satan, and the antichrist, preparing themselves for the short time in which they will have control of our world.

This time will be precisely 3 and 1/2 years, so even though we will go through this time of great trouble, it will only be short when we consider eternity with our Father and His Son and His Holy Spirit.

Revelation 16:13-14 says:

> [13] And I saw three unclean spirits like frogs *coming* out of the mouth of the dragon, out of the mouth of the beast, and out of the mouth of the false prophet. [14] For they are spirits of demons, performing signs, *which* go out to the kings of the Earth and of the whole world, to gather them to the battle of that great day of God Almighty.

We know Who wins this battle between the Almighty and the unholy trinity made up of Satan, the antichrist, and the false prophet. Rev 19:20 tells us:

> [20] Then the beast was captured, and with him the false prophet who worked signs in his presence, by which he deceived those who received the mark of the beast and those who worshiped his image. These two were cast alive into the lake of fire burning with brimstone.

Our founders fought tirelessly against soul-destroying doctrines and theologies that were creeping into the body of Christ in this first century A.D. Paul fought battle after battle with the Jewish leaders who were trying to force Jewish customs upon new believers and thus watering down the price that Jesus had paid for their sins on the cross.

John had to fight for the fact that Jesus came in the flesh and lived among us, whereas people said it was all a mirage, a reflection of His appearing.

Jude and Paul again warned us about false teachers, false prophets, and false apostles, transforming themselves to masquerade and hide their true intention, which was to destroy the Church.

Every writer of the New Testament paid the supreme price for the Truth with their lives (John excepted), being martyred because they would not compromise the Truth. Can we even begin to imagine how many lies, how much heretical teaching, and how much soul-destroying doctrine has now been accepted by the greater Church? We could multiply the first century by 20 times and still come up short.

My Burden

I have a burden that the Lord has placed on my heart over many years working on the front line in several countries and with many denominations witnessing "the real and the fake," the "kingdom builders, and the *personal* kingdom builders." This burden compelled me to write this book, born out of necessity for the true Church to see the true God in all His fullness. Not the hearsay and traditions that have come about over the centuries and have painted the Father, Son, and Holy Spirit in such an obscure, unrecognizable light that They can no longer be recognized for Their full majesty and sovereignty and the glory they rightly deserve.

We must understand how the world perceives God; the only filter they have through which to see Him is the Church, which has portrayed a highly distorted view of Who He truly is. The doctrines of religion that have been shown to the world by the fake churches have so distorted the image of the One True GOD and have turned people away. He has now become unrecognizable as the True Being He actually is.

There are so many fables, pictures, and fairytales, as people have plucked out and twisted Scripture out of context to either make a mockery of God or, worse, make an image of the god they would like to believe He is, pushing their views onto others to make them believe.

The Holy Bible

The Holy Bible is unlike any other book ever written in that it is the only Book ever produced that is alive. This unique Book of books tells us how this world came to be and how it will ultimately end. A whole new world and universe will be created, and all will be brought into being by none other than Jesus Christ Himself.

The Bible contains hundreds and hundreds of prophecies that have come to pass to the letter, plus many unfulfilled prophecies that will also come to pass in the same manner. It is filled with poetry written thousands of years ago that is more relevant today than when it was first written. It is a Book that covers every relationship known to man and how to live out these relationships. It is our world's history and a Book of the present and future. What a Book! It is from this Book that my book has sprung. Everything I know comes from the powerful Word of God.

Replacement Theology

Here, in the last chapter of my book, I need to address a huge problem, and that problem has a name: Replacement Theology. Due to the amount of rubbish in the form of false teaching that has been fed into our fellowships over 2,000 years and then devoured by the modern western churches, particularly within the last 50 years, we have been all led to the cliff face, and we are now teetering on it.

Replacement Theology usually refers to the false idea that the Church has replaced Israel, becoming the new chosen people. But I define Replacement Theology differently. It is not that the Church has replaced Israel, but that we, the people, the churchgoers, have replaced Jesus as the Head of the Church. In short, we have dethroned Him and put ourselves in His place. *We* are now self-governing and the focus in the vast majority of our churches.

Stop and take note when you attend your next church meeting. Weigh up how much time and effort are spent on us, the congregation, compared to the effort put into building our relationships with the Father, Son, and Holy Spirit, with Them being the focus.

How much conversation before and after each meeting is centered on our One True God compared to the time we call fellowship discussing every mundane world event or our favorite social media podcast? Almost every song that is sung each Sunday is all about "us," "I," "me," "we," and "our." Every sermon follows the same format: We have taken the spotlight of Jesus Christ and placed it on ourselves so that it has now reached the point that a fake Jesus is accepted within the churches that it makes God want to vomit because we have become so lukewarm. (Revelation 3)

When I did missionary work in the Philippines, we encountered many different denominations that believe in eight different types of Jesus. Just look at how many non-scriptural versions of Jesus are being preached today in our churches. Where would we be today if the true Christ had been revealed to the world by the Church?

Would we have a world on the brink of destruction because of people who have been allowed to gain control and are convinced that they are in control? In fact, they are being controlled by demonic forces. But when we consider the omnipotence of the Father, Son, and Holy Spirit, we know Who is really in the driver's seat and will have the final say in every matter. God's plan is already set in concrete. The only changes that will occur concern those to be included in His plan.

Hell

Hell is the *unconstrained man.* Can you begin to imagine spending eternity with someone that you detest, and you can't get away from? That is another version of Hell–where God does not dwell.

Our world is now experiencing a taste of Hell and what is to come for those who do not have Jesus as their first love. This taste of Hell is going to become more and more pungent and bitter as we watch our world spiral into the abyss.

Up to two-thirds of the world's population will perish, according to prophetic Scripture. Read Isaiah 24. These Scriptures paint the most graphic picture down to the last detail of what will happen to our fallen world. We have pushed God out of our churches, and that has resulted in having God pushed out of our societies. We live daily with these consequences and have them thrust upon our children. When we push God away, He simply leaves us to our own devices—man in control of man will prove to be catastrophic.

As of this writing, it seems the whole world is on the offensive against Israel. This latest attack on God's people, especially by Hamas, provides us with the most horrific pictures and a display of the level that man will sink to when he is unrestrained by God. We are witnessing a fight between good and evil, right and wrong. How callous can a heart become when it is under the control of the adversary?

Our early church fathers warned us that people would creep into our fellowships and teach the brethren to be disobedient to Christ and fall out of love with Him by not obeying His commandments. (1 Tim 6:3-5)

Jesus told us, "If you love Me you will obey My commandments. If you don't love Me, then you won't." (John 14 to 17) When we first come to Christ, there is an immediate heart connection, and if we nurture that connection, then Jesus will make the love grow deeper and deeper. But sadly, what has happened is we are being spoon-fed by self-elevating wolves in sheep's clothing wanting to feather their own nests and lift themselves up with wealth, applause, and adulation, seeking the chief seats and the honor of men, all to the detriment of the Church and the entire human race.

It's About Jesus Christ

The Church has to be entirely about Jesus Christ. Only then will our lives be set in order and our relationships with family and each other be as they should be. We have never before faced such a set of political dominoes set in place. Here are just a few of the demonic social ideas taking hold:

The Great Reset

There are powerful people on the Earth who want to see seven and a half billion people eradicated and a new way of global living. Led by Klaus Schwab and the World Economic Forum, their plans, some openly discussed, and some kept secret, fit neatly into apocalyptic Scripture and will likely figure into the drama of the end times.

China

A careful reading of Revelations 9 and 16 causes me to believe China is going to kill one-third of humankind in some sort of warfare. Read all of Chapter 9, especially verses 13-19. This passage even describes our modern-day missiles and says this army of 200,000,000 will kill a third of mankind.

The colors described caught me off guard for some time because they are in prominence firstly Red, and Blue, and lastly, yellow. The colors of the Chinese air force and navy are exactly these colors in these dimensions.

It is also worth combining this with Revelation 16:12-14 (please read). I did a work on the Trumpets, Seals, and Bowls in Revelation and, though it took some time, I laid them out like this:

Seal 1, Trumpet 1, Bowl 1

I then did that with all seven and it was incredible how they fitted into each other. What I believe John saw in the Heavenly Throne Room was like what we see in earthly royal courts. The King breaks the seal making a decree. An angel then blows a trumpet announcing the decree, then another angel acts on that decree, pouring out the bowl of God's wrath.

When I did this, it provided me with a timeline, but not the actual timing of the events so we are told what will happen next and what we should expect to see.

Islam

There is a theocratic religion in authority over the Middle East whose stated aim is the death of all Christians and those "infidel" countries where Christianity exists. Islamic terrorists are not the outliers; they are the governments themselves.

Artificial Intelligence

On top of all of this, we rush on with A.I., which is the absolute pinnacle of lunacy, with even one of the leading proponents, Elon Musk, telling us this is the greatest threat ever to civilization as he helps to perpetuate its spread. On our farm, I have a lot to do with heavy earth-moving equipment, and it occurs to me what these large machines are capable of in the wrong hands. Remember what one terrorist did with one small truck, not to mention what a handful of terrorists did with a couple of aircraft on 9/11. What will happen if A.I. is in charge of the computers of these vehicles?

What will happen when the majority of the population gets computer chips implanted in their brains? It is unlikely that anyone will ever force anyone to do it. It will be an economic decision willingly made by the masses.

If we had not replaced Jesus in our churches with ourselves, would we now have transvestites and drag queens reading stories to our precious children in our libraries, or worse, preaching behind the pulpit? Would child trafficking and exploitation have taken over as a higher income generator in America than even the sale of drugs? Sin and evil are gripping our world in epic proportions, the likes of which this Earth has never witnessed.

False Doctrines

Whenever we face any question, decision, or theological doctrine, we all need to stop and ask: Is this from the flesh, or is it from Jesus, and then is this doctrine confirmed in His Word? If not, we should immediately discard it.

We have to stop going with the flow, with the crowd, and instead, we need to know our Bibles intimately, particularly the Words of Jesus Christ, so that no one can pull the wolf's skin over our eyes. Jesus could foresee what is now happening 2,000 years ago when He asked if He would "find faith on the Earth" when He returns. (Lk 18:8)

I was once in a group discussion, and we read this passage. A young Christian girl piped up with, "He can't say that." That was blasphemous talk, but because of the condition of the Church and its teaching, this has now produced Christians who feel entitled to reach this level of replacing Christ with themselves and their own opinions and self-importance.

Not very long ago, saints would not dare question the Word of Jesus. Now, His Words are tossed about so lightly, challenged, and debated as though they were just the writings of a normal human being. His Word is not receiving the awe and respect that should be given to the Divine Son of God. Jesus is the "Word made flesh." (Jn 1:14) How can we become so flippant about Him and His Word? Here are the most widely accepted false doctrines destroying our churches today.

The Unconditional Love of God and Jesus

When the unconditional love of God is preached, what is really being preached and taught is the *nonjudgmental Jesus*. "He will never judge me." Then, it is implied that God should not be allowed to have His freewill. He must love everyone because we say so, so our place in Heaven is secure. Our insurance policy is all paid up.

Then, people who believe this give the game away by making derogatory statements about people that they don't like, showing how they feel about those who have been created in the image of God. But Jesus is not allowed this same privilege of freewill.

Some denominations have even gone as far as to rewrite their Bibles, removing the fear of God and Hell and all its consequences, all in the name of being men-pleasers and growing churches.

I have even heard the statement, "Jesus never offended anyone." I don't know what Bible they are reading, but mine reads that He offended nearly everyone, even His mother and brothers, to the point of stating that only they who do His Father's will are His mother, brothers, and sisters. Jesus would not have been killed were He not so offensive.

I just keep hearing over and over again, "God loves everyone." "God hates sin but loves the sinner." How do you love someone when You are spewing them out of your mouth? How do you love someone that is an abomination to You? How do you love someone that disgusts You

Romans 9:13 says: "As it is written, 'Jacob I have loved, but Esau I have hated.'" This is talking about the son of Isaac. Leviticus 26:30 says: "I will destroy your high places, cut down your incense altars, and cast your carcasses on the lifeless forms of your idols; and My soul shall abhor you." These are the children of Israel, God's chosen people.

And yet when we read about the Church of Laodicea in Revelation 3:19, which was one of the two churches out of the seven in Asia about which Jesus did not have one good word to say, (the other was Sardis) "As many as I love, I rebuke and chasten. Therefore, be zealous and repent."

Here, Jesus plainly says that He still loves them, and that is why He is chastening them, directing them to repentance so that they can get back into their broken relationships. Can you love and hate another person at the same time? I am not talking about hating and yet lusting after simultaneously; these are human emotions. I mean deep emotional love and hate. Only God can have perfect love and, simultaneously, perfect hatred because He alone is perfect. We get lost when we endeavor to come to terms with these concepts. They are so far above our thinking that we are all just wading in the shallows. "For now, we see in a mirror, dimly, but then face to face. Now I know in part, but then I shall know just as I also am known." (1 Cor 13:12)

His ways are so far above ours and beyond human comprehension. Why do we fail to understand the true meaning of love and hate? It is because we have not only completely distorted the meaning of love, but we have also done the same thing with hate. We toss these two words of the epitome of relationship around so loosely that they have now lost all true meaning.

The Sinner's Prayer

We have been provided with the McDonald's salvation message, telling people just to give their hearts to the Lord, make a decision for Christ, say the sinner's prayer.

We need to go no further than the Words of our Lord and King. He, at the very start of His ministry, began with this opening statement, "You need to repent," then He followed that up with, "You must be born from above by being born of water and the Spirit to not only enter the Kingdom of God but even to see it."

The very first step on the road to salvation is repentance. How can a new believer take the next steps of belief, water baptism, and spirit baptism without having first repented? How often and how many of these four necessary steps of salvation are being preached in our churches? Paul cut to the chase in Acts 26:19-20:

> [19] "Therefore, King Agrippa, I was not disobedient to the heavenly vision, [20] but declared first to those in Damascus and in Jerusalem, and throughout all the region of Judea, and *then* to the Gentiles, that they should repent, turn to God, and do works befitting repentance." (NKJV)

A salvation without repentance is no salvation at all. It is a failure to understand sin, the consequences of sin, and the price Christ paid for our redemption. He died for us to repent, so we must do it.

Pre-Tribulation Rapture

The secret pre-tribulation rapture teaching is broadly accepted by the greater body of the Church, saying that we saints will all escape the great tribulation that is about to come on our Earth. This teaching makes a complete mockery of the Words of Jesus. His Words alone are enough to debunk this man-pleasing ideology and require no further argument. One only needs to read Matthew 24:23-31:

> [23] Then, if anyone says to you, "Look, here *is* the Christ!" or "There!" do not believe it. [24] For false Christs and prophets will rise and show great signs and wonders to deceive, if possible, even the elect. [25] See, I have told you beforehand.
>
> [26] Therefore, if they say to you, "Look, He is in the desert!" do not go out; *or* "Look, *He is* in the inner rooms!" do not believe

it. [27] For as the lightning comes from the east and flashes to the west, so also will the coming of the Son of Man be. [28] For wherever the carcass is, there the eagles will be gathered.

[29] Immediately after the tribulation of those days, the sun will be darkened, and the moon will not give its light; the stars will fall from Heaven, and the powers of the heavens will be shaken. [30] Then the sign of the Son of Man will appear in Heaven, and then all the tribes of the Earth will mourn, and they will see the Son of Man coming on the clouds of Heaven with power and great glory. [31] And He will send His angels with a great sound of a trumpet, and they will gather His elect from the four winds, from one end of Heaven to the other. (NKJV Emphasis added)

Mark 13:21-27 confirms the Words of Jesus. If this is what Jesus had to say on this subject, then ask who would dare to call Jesus a liar or say He does not know what He is talking about. He has made it clear as day, and this topic does not need further argument.

[21] Then if anyone says to you, "Look, here *is* the Christ!" or, "Look, *He is* there!" do not believe it. [2] For false Christs and false prophets will rise and show signs and wonders to deceive, if possible, even the elect. [23] But, take heed; see, I have told you all things beforehand.

[24] But in those days, after that tribulation, the sun will be darkened, and the moon will not give its light; [25] the stars of Heaven will fall, and the powers in the heavens will be shaken. [26] Then they will see the Son of Man coming in the clouds with great power and glory. [27] And then He will send His angels and gather His elect from the four winds, from the farthest part of Earth to the farthest part of Heaven.

We Christians need to tread ever so lightly when we start to think about misrepresenting the Words of Jesus. He is the Word. To twist something that is this holy is the epitome of folly.

False Ways of Receiving the Holy Spirit

There have become so many theological interpretations on receiving the Holy Spirit that I can't keep up with all of them. All these are false doctrines implemented without considering how much offense is laid at the feet of the only One Who can truly baptize in the Holy Spirit.

Again, we have chosen to please man rather than please God. Simply read the four accounts we are provided with in our Scriptures: Acts 2, Acts 8, Acts 10 and 11, Acts 19. To lay the proper foundation, let's again take the exact Words of our Lord, not adding to nor taking away from them.

Jesus, speaking in the chapters of John 14 to 17, says that the Holy Spirit "cannot come until I go to My Father." (Jn 16:7)

It all started on the Day of Pentecost (Acts 2), and it has never changed. Neither has the evidence (speaking in tongues). Jesus is the same yesterday, today, and forever. Paul tells us in Galatians 3:14, "that the blessing of Abraham might come upon the Gentiles in Christ Jesus, that we might receive the promise of the Spirit through faith."

Paul is telling us that receiving the Holy Spirit can only come through faith in Christ as Lord and complete surrender to His will, as only He can baptize anyone with the Holy Spirit. It doesn't matter how many good works you may have done, or how many theological degrees you may have under your belt.

And it must be understood from Scripture that the Baptism of the Holy Spirit is never automatic. You only need to read Luke 11:1 to 13. Christ only gives the Holy Spirit to those who reach that point of complete surrender and obedience to Him through continually knocking, asking, and seeking. With some new believers, this can come instantly, and with others, it can take years. God knows the heart and the timing.

Eternal Security

"Once saved, always saved" and "Free grace." These can only come from the pit of Hell. As I mentioned in a previous chapter, the Bible clearly refutes this. I searched the whole New Testament and found 104 references referring directly to Christians, telling us our salvation can be forfeited.

To be charitable, I will say that some hold to the doctrine out of reverence for God. They understand His work to be irrevocable and themselves as being so dependent on Him that they could not defy His "irresistible grace." The problem is that this is nonsensical and unbiblical. I can make these 104 Scriptural references available to anyone who asks. The two most prominent books are Matthew and Hebrews. There are 19 references in Matthew, and in the book to the Hebrews, there are 15.

Some will say that if one leaves the faith, they were never of it. While there is a verse to support this (1 Jn), I don't believe it outweighs the others. We should always beware that we can leave God and turn back to the world. The Bible lovingly warns us incessantly against doing so.

The Prosperity Gospel

Where does one begin with this dreadful doctrine? Well, let's look at the tragedy of Ananias and Sapphira in Acts 5, who lied when giving money to the Church deceitfully. Look at the offense God took to what they had done: the two are dead on the spot.

If God is so offended by the wrong giving, how do we think He feels about someone stealing money in the name of Christ? Can we comprehend how angry God becomes when church leaders deceitfully, do not give, but *take money from the most vulnerable and innocent* to line their own pockets, claiming that God will provide them with more money because these poor souls have funded the mansions and private jets of the false teachers?

Who would want to be in their shoes when Jesus asks them, "Do I know you? And do you know Me?"

Women in Church Authority

I have the greatest admiration for women, and as an employer over many years and employing hundreds of men and women, my preference is to employ women; they are more loyal and faithful, and they don't steal from you.

We read in Luke 8 that the women supported our Lord's ministry. Moreover, look at the last week of the life of Christ. The women didn't betray Him. They did not desert Him. They were the ones with Him at the crucifixion, and the women were the first ones at the tomb.

To see the root cause behind this issue, we have to go back to the beginning in Genesis 3:16. God puts His decree and order in place, but the rebellious hearts harden past the point of being equal in value and dignity is not enough. Women push and push until they have control over the men.

> To the woman, He said: "I will greatly multiply your sorrow and your conception; In pain you shall bring forth children; Your desire shall be for your husband, and he shall rule over you." (Gen 3:16)

God has given a precise order; in this order, all things exist.

God is male: Father and Son, male and male. Jesus and His Church? Male Leader and female follower. Whenever this order is fought against, no good can come from it. We see so many cults that have arisen out of this rebellion.

Let's try to settle the matter by asking some straightforward factual questions, and then the floor is open.

1. In our Bibles and the history of humanity, what was the first account of a woman taking the headship/lead over the man? Is it not in the Garden of Eden when Eve succumbed to the enemy's wiles, ate the fruit first, and then gave it to Adam to eat so that she could share the guilt? How has that worked out?

2. Today, more women leaders are in our world than ever. Is the world a better place?

3. Not one word in our Bibles has been written by a woman. The Bible is a library of 66 books with 40 authors, 39 of whom were Jews and 1 Gentile, none of whom is a woman. I once put this question to a woman raised by a matriarchal mother and a passive father. She responded, "Yes, and that is the problem; the Bible is written by men."

Jesus chose all His apostles to build and lead His Church, all males.

Finally, look again at God's divine order. God-Son, Father-Son, male-male, then we have GOD - Israel, male leadership, female submission under this leadership.
JESUS - Church, male leadership, female submission under this leadership
Husband - Wife, male leadership, female submission to this leadership. Whenever this divine order is broken, no good can come of it.
All the laws of the universe are encapsulated in this one order.

> [2] Now, I praise you, brethren, that you remember me in all things and keep the traditions just as I delivered *them* to you. [3] But, I want you to know that the Head of every man is Christ, the head of woman *is* man, and the Head of Christ *is* God. (1 Cor 11:2-3)

God is the Head of Christ (male), Who is the Head of the Church (female). Christ (male) is the Head of the man (male), who is the head of his wife (female). This is the biblical order.

These are just some of the many false doctrines in the Church today, with more introduced daily. We need to steer away from them; they are quicksand that will suck one in because, like the fruit eaten in the Garden of Eden, they look "pleasant to the eyes," and they appeal to our fallen nature. All these invented doctrines are dangerous territory for a saint and have robbed so many of their eternal salvation.

No denomination has clean hands in these. We have all contributed over the years, some to a higher, and some to a lesser degree. All these infiltrated doctrines are all about us and have come from the enemy, not from Jesus or His Words.

We desperately need to hand Christ His Church back before it is too late.

Look at the awe and respect that each of the writers of our New Testament and early founders of the Church applied and how they disciplined themselves when they wrote the New Testament.

See how carefully they push themselves out of the picture so that all the glory, honor, and worship would go directly to the One Who has done it all.

Have you noticed that in the four gospels, the author would barely even mention his own name out of pure respect for the Lord? They did not want to detract in the slightest from the Son of Man.

Look at some of the other writers:

James (1:1) calls himself a slave of God and His Son, Jesus Christ. "James, a bondservant." This is the only mention of his name in the entire epistle.

Jude 1:1 says: "Jude, a bondservant of Jesus Christ, and brother of James. To those who are called, sanctified by God the Father, and preserved in Jesus Christ:"

Both devout men were the brothers of Jesus but would dare not mention this fact. They felt it would be treading on holy ground and would take something special away from that which only belongs to the Godhead were they to name-drop in that way.

Luke, when he wrote the Book of Acts of the Holy Spirit, did not make one mention of his own name.

And consider the book of Hebrews. To this day, we still do not know who wrote this book. Out of holy reverence for God, the author would not dare draw any attention to himself and apply his name to it.

What has happened now is we want all the attention centered on us. Where do we get off, and how dare we do the opposite of these great men of God?

We want to make ourselves feel bigger, elevating ourselves and drawing on the praise and adoration of others. Well, Jesus said you have your reward, and that is all you will get.

With the rise of social media, it is getting worse day by day; the whole world revolves around and exists entirely for the individual's benefit. This "I, me" attitude has sneaked into the churches. Godly writers warned us this would happen and that we would not accept the fullness of Christ and His Divinity. Jesus also warned us in Matthew 11:6, saying, "And blessed is he who is not offended because of Me."

He knew that the true Savior's Words would offend many. Just give it a try at your church. Try preaching just the Words of Jesus and watch the reactions this will draw.

When have you ever heard these Scriptures preached in any setting—church, social media, tele-preachers—they are the Words of our Lord and Sovereign King. Why don't we preach them?

Luke 12:49-53 says:

> [49] I came to send fire on the Earth, and how I wish it were already kindled! [50] But I have a baptism to be baptized with, and how distressed I am till it is accomplished! [51] Do *you* suppose that I came to give peace on Earth? I tell you, not at all, but rather division. [52] For from now on five in one house will be divided: three against two, and two against three. [53] Father will be divided against son and son against father, mother against daughter and daughter against mother, mother-in-law against her daughter-in-law and daughter-in-law against her mother-in-law. (NKJV)

I have chosen here *not* to focus on His love, mercy, grace, and forgiveness, which are all as infinite as is His Being, because we, the Church, have so warped His image, and now we live in a world that has absolutely no fear or reverence for the omnipotent God. Therefore, there is no fear of standing before Him in judgment.

Throughout all these subjects, I have repeatedly tried to lay a foundation on which to build a life worthy of the sacrifice that has been paid for each of us. I have done this so we can understand the selfless *agape* love freely given by the Father and the Son and then rightfully apply the love of Jesus as we read in 1 Corinthians 13. These 15 unique character traits only belong to the One. Every one of His holy attributes are conditional and belong to Him alone.

Look Upon Jesus

Stop and take a breath; look closely at the Person, Jesus Christ. You will find it refreshing and give you strength that will allow you to release your*self* into true freedom when you realize your Defender, your Rock, is this divine, awesome, omnipotent Son of God.

Jesus will awe you, inspiring the due respect for His Sovereignty and Majesty, and He will give you His faith and love.

He will teach you to fall into the most profound love with Him, which our pure, sweet Savior rightfully deserves, but you have to take the entire package: the goodness and the severity of God, not just an image we want to paint for ourselves of the god we want Him to be. These images we form in our minds become no different from any other idol fashioned by man in man's own image. Then, we are left with a weak, flexible, movable, changeable god we can control and, therefore, cannot be relied on when it really matters.

So often, we hear about the unconditional love of Jesus and the love of Jesus for everybody and how He would never send anyone to Hell. But the truth is that everything we know about Hell came from the lips of Jesus Himself. No other writer would have been credentialed enough to share these gruesome depictions.

We must believe in the fullness of the Christ Who came to save the world from its sin, which is taking them to Hell, so that we can restore the fear and reverence for the One Who has the strength and capacity to save them from Hell.

A valid realization of the Absolute Jesus Who is returning to this Earth to set things right, is found in Revelation 6:15-17:

> [15] And the kings of the Earth, the great men, the rich men, the commanders, the mighty men, every slave, and every free man, hid themselves in the caves and in the rocks of the mountains, [16] and said to the mountains and rocks, "Fall on us and hide us from the face of Him Who sits on the throne and from the

wrath of the Lamb! [17] For the great day of His wrath has come, and who is able to stand?"

Revelation 19:11-21 says:

[11] Now I saw Heaven opened, and behold, a white horse. And He Who sat on him *was* called faithful and true, and in righteousness He judges and makes war. [12] His eyes *were* like a flame of fire, and on His head *were* many crowns. He had a name written that no one knew except Himself. [13] He *was* clothed with a robe dipped in blood, and His name is called the Word of God. [14] And the armies in Heaven, clothed in fine linen, white and clean, followed Him on white horses. [15] Now out of His mouth goes a sharp sword, that with it He should strike the nations. And He Himself will rule them with a rod of iron. He Himself treads the winepress of the fierceness and wrath of Almighty God. [16] And He has on *His* robe and on His thigh a name written:

KING OF KINGS AND
LORD OF LORDS.

[17] Then I saw an angel standing in the sun; and he cried with a loud voice, saying to all the birds that fly in the midst of Heaven, "Come and gather for the supper of the great God, [18] that you may eat the flesh of kings, the flesh of captains, the flesh of mighty men, the flesh of horses and of those who sit on them, and the flesh of all *people,* free and slave, both small and great."

[19] And I saw the beast, the kings of the Earth, and their armies, gathered to make war against Him Who sat on the horse and against His army. [20] Then the beast was captured, and with him the false prophet who worked signs in his presence, by which he deceived those who received the mark of the beast and those

who worshiped his image. These two were cast alive into the lake of fire burning with brimstone. [21] And the rest were killed with the sword which proceeded from the mouth of Him Who sat on the horse. And all the birds were filled with their flesh.

Before this, we heard from the prophets, including Isaiah, who wrote in Isaiah 63:1-6:

> [1] Who *is* this who comes from Edom, With dyed garments from Bozrah, This *One who is* glorious in His apparel, Traveling in the greatness of His strength? — "I who speak in righteousness, mighty to save." [2] Why *is* Your apparel red, And Your garments like one who treads in the winepress? [3] "I have trodden the winepress alone, And from the peoples, no one *was* with Me. For I have trodden them in My anger, And trampled them in My fury; Their blood is sprinkled upon My garments, And I have stained all My robes. [4] For the day of vengeance *is* in My heart, And the year of My redeemed has come. [5] I looked, but *there was* no one to help, And I wondered That *there was* no one to uphold; Therefore, My own arm brought salvation for Me; And My own fury, it sustained Me. [6] I have trodden down the peoples in My anger, Made them drunk in My fury, And brought down their strength to the Earth." (NKJV)

I have heard Christian brothers and sisters make comments in discussion about a preacher who applied the Word of God factually, and their comments were something like: "This guy/preacher said Jesus is going to kill people, and that is not true."

In the book of Revelation alone, it says that when Jesus returns to our Earth, He will slay hundreds of millions of people with the sword of His mouth. One army He will destroy will consist of 200,000,000, and our Bibles tell us that all the armies of the world will come against Israel, so how many will Jesus actually slay? We don't know.

Zechariah 12:2-4 says:

> [2] "Behold, I will make Jerusalem a cup of drunkenness to all the surrounding peoples, when they lay siege against Judah and Jerusalem. [3] And it shall happen in that day that I will make Jerusalem a very heavy stone for all peoples; all who would heave it away will surely be cut in pieces, though all nations of the Earth are gathered against it. [4] In that day," says the LORD, "I will strike every horse with confusion, and its rider with madness; I will open My eyes on the house of Judah and strike every horse of the peoples with blindness." (NKJV)

Verses 9-10 tell us:

> [9] It shall be in that day that I will seek to destroy all the nations that come against Jerusalem. [10] And I will pour on the house of David and on the inhabitants of Jerusalem the Spirit of grace and supplication; then they will look on Me Whom they pierced. Yes, they will mourn for Him as one mourns for his only son, and grieve for Him as one grieves for a firstborn. (NKJV)

Zechariah 14:1-4 says:

> [1] Behold, the Day of the LORD is coming, And your spoil will be divided in your midst. [2] For I will gather all the nations to battle against Jerusalem; The city shall be taken, The houses rifled, And the women ravished. Half of the city shall go into captivity, But the remnant of the people shall not be cut off from the city. [3] Then the LORD will go forth and fight against those nations, As He fights in the day of battle. [4] And in that day His feet will stand on the Mount of Olives, Which faces Jerusalem on the east. And the Mount of Olives shall be split in two, From east to west, *Making* a very large valley; Half of the mountain shall move toward the north And half of it toward the south. (NKJV)

Verse 9 says: "And the Lord shall be King over all the Earth. In that day it shall be— "The Lord is one, and His name one.""

Verses:12-13,15 tells us:

> [12] And this shall be the plague with which the LORD will strike all the people who fought against Jerusalem: Their flesh shall dissolve while they stand on their feet, Their eyes shall dissolve in their sockets, And their tongues shall dissolve in their mouths. [13] It shall come to pass in that day *That* a great panic from the LORD will be among them. Everyone will seize the hand of his neighbor, And raise his hand against his neighbor's hand; [15] Such also shall be the plague, On the horse *and* the mule, On the camel and the donkey, And on all the cattle that will be in those camps. So *shall* this plague *be*. (NKJV)

We have the love of God over-preached to a world without comprehension of what true love is. They do not understand 1 Corinthians 13 and could never begin to appreciate the price paid for them. We must do and say what Jesus did and said and start with repentance.

John 12:32 says: "And I, if I am lifted from the Earth, will draw all peoples to Myself."

Job 34:14-15 says:

> [14] If He should set His heart on it, *If* He should gather to Himself His Spirit and His breath, [15] All flesh would perish together, And man would return to dust.

Let's go and be faithful to God and His Word, His Son, and His Holy Spirit, and preach true repentance, true love, and a true gospel, and save as many as we can until He returns and it is too late. If you need to repent, repent! Come to Him and let Him send you with His true message of repentance and peace.

YAHWEH

"He in Whom all creation have their being."

ACKNOWLEDGEMENTS

Over many years of being on the front line, I have endeavored to be obedient to my LORD JESUS CHRIST by doing and saying what I believed HE asked me to do and say. Therefore, the real Author of this book is Jesus Christ, "HE" is the Word of God.

I would like to thank my friend Jeff Miller, whose invaluable input and writing skills have helped me pull this book together and meet the deadlines for the publisher. Thank you, Jeff.

David Pawson, whose messages went out into the whole world encouraging Christians to know and understand the Bible and their relationships with Its Author—the Father and His Holy Spirit more perfectly. David has been inspirational in helping me dig deeper into the holy Word of God.

Our dear friends, John and Jean Spall, for their encouragement and support and just being there on and off the mission fields, and who to this day continue to work tirelessly in the work of the Lord.

My wife/one body, mere words cannot express her loyalty and perseverance throughout the most difficult times we have gone through together. She is my second great love and all of my earthly treasure.

Our three wonderful children Mitch, Nat, and Isaac, of whom I am so proud to be their father. They have remained steadfast in CHRIST and raised our eight precious grandchildren, who also are growing in CHRIST day by day. They have kept me humble and my feet on the ground.

Made in the USA
Middletown, DE
27 May 2024

54912569R00155